The McGraw-Hill Guide to Starting Your Own Business

The McGraw-Hill Guide to Starting Your Own Business

A Step-by-Step Blueprint for the First-Time Entrepreneur

Stephen C. Harper

McGraw-Hill, Inc.

New York St. Louis San Francisco Auckland Bogotá
Caracas Hamburg Lisbon London Madrid
Mexico Milan Montreal New Delhi Paris
San Juan São Paulo Singapore
Sydney Tokyo Toronto

Library of Congress Cataloging-in-Publication Data

Harper, Stephen C.
    The McGraw-Hill guide to starting your own business : a step-by-
step blueprint for the first-time entrepreneur / Stephen C. Harper.
        p.   cm.
    Includes index.
    ISBN 0-07-026685-9
    1. New business enterprises.   I. Title.
HD62.5.H3734   1991
658.1'141—dc20   90-44711
                                                                      CIP

*The sponsoring editor for this book was James H. Bessent, Jr., the editing
supervisor was Alfred Bernardi, the designer was Naomi Auerbach, and the
production supervisor was Suzanne W. Babeuf. It was set in Baskerville by
McGraw-Hill's Professional Publishing composition unit.*

Printed and bound by R. R. Donnelley & Sons Company.

This book is dedicated to:

America—The Land of Opportunity.

The entrepreneurs—who have had the courage of their convictions to venture out and create the standard of living we enjoy today.

My students, who demonstrate the spirit is alive.

My father, H. Mitchell Harper, Jr., who helped me realize you can't take it with you and that life is not a spectator sport.

The people who came up with the Schlitz slogan, "If you can only go around once in life, then do it with gusto!" and the Michelob slogan, "Who said you can't have it all?" These sayings capture the essence of the entrepreneurial spirit.

Contents

Part 2. Preparing Your Business Plan

3. The General Overview and Legal Structure   49

4. Selecting the Right Target Market   69

5. Product-Service Strategy and Price Strategy   85

Part 3. The ABCs of Financing and Alternatives to Starting From Scratch

Preface

The McGraw-Hill Guide to Starting Your Own Business has been written for the same reason most businesses are started . . . to fill a void in the marketplace. Numerous books are available about starting a business. However, few books are tailored to people who have limited experience and education in business. Some books are too simplistic. They try to be funny, offer few guidelines on how to actually start a business, and paint too rosy a picture. Other books assume the reader has a MBA from Harvard and plans to start a high-technology business with venture capital.

This guide is written for the "first-timer." It is not intended to encourage or discourage the reader from starting a business. Instead, it is designed to show that while starting a business can be a mentally stimulating and financially rewarding endeavor, it can also be a time-consuming, demanding, and risky undertaking. *Starting Your Own Business* encourages readers to take an objective look at what is involved in starting a business as well as at themselves to be sure they have what it takes to succeed. It's a step-by-step guide that goes from identifying business opportunities all the way to providing the information needed for getting a loan. Starting a business is similar to embarking on a long journey, a journey where the odds are that, unfortunately, most people will fail. Eight out of ten businesses started this year will not be around in ten years. Only one of the ten will make a significant profit. This book serves as the first-timer's guide for starting a business that will beat the odds!

Acknowledgments

This book was partly the result of a faculty research grant provided by the Cameron School of Business Administration at the University of North Carolina in Wilmington. This grant made it possible for me to take some time off from my regular activities to sit down and map out this book. Eight people associated with UNC-Wilmington deserve special recognition—Jane Kenan, who, as an MBA candidate, provided considerable editorial and research assistance, as well as Elaine Ferguson (now at Randolph-Macon College), Carolyn Cook, Rhonda LaMarsh, Barbara Holder, Susan Ritz, Amy Brown, and Trudy Owen, all of whom provided valuable editorial and secretarial assistance. Their quick turnaround time placed the responsibility for completing this manuscript in my lap. I also want to thank all the people who have worked with me over the years on our annual workshop, "Starting a Small Business." Six people should be acknowledged: Dr. Earl Honeycutt, Associate Professor of Marketing at UNC-Wilmington; Mr. Ted Jans, Director of the Southeast Regional Service Center for the North Carolina Small Business and Technology Development Center; Mr. H. Charles Craft, III, C.P.A., and Partner in Cherry, Bekaert & Holland C.P.A.; Mr. Ernie Sewell, Senior Vice President of Branch Bank and Trust Company (BB&T); Dr. Jim Edmundson, Director of the Office of Special Programs at UNC-Wilmington; and Mr. David Lewis, J.D., who is in private practice with Wishant, Norris, Henringer, P.A. in Burlington, North Carolina. Charles, Ted, David, and Tom Long, President of Maricultura Inc., also provided valuable editorial assistance.

Stephen C. Harper

The McGraw-Hill Guide to Starting Your Own Business

PART 1

Prerequisites for Start-Up Survival and Success

Introduction— There Are No Guarantees for Success

Profit Is the Reward for Beating the Odds

The fact that you opened this book indicates you are contemplating starting a new business. You may be among the readers who have already decided to start a business. All you need to do is determine what type of business to start, how large it should be, where it should be located, how much money it will take, how it can be financed, and when will be the best time to start it. Conversely, you could be among the readers who are merely curious about what may be involved in starting a new business.

Whether you are at the point where you can't eat, drink, or sleep without thinking about starting your own business or just toying with the notion of starting a business "sometime" in your life, one thing is clear...starting a business, even a small one, is a major undertaking. It is not like taking up a hobby or going on a diet. Nor is it a glamorous form of semiretirement. Starting a business is a serious endeavor and it requires considerable preparation.

Many people view starting a business as comparable to embarking on a glorious adventure, filled with challenge and excitement. Yet, if you ask people who started their first business in the last couple of years how they feel about it now, many will tell you the honeymoon lasted only a few weeks, the marriage has involved considerable anxiety and self-sacrifice, and they continue to wonder if they should get a divorce from the business! Most of the people who have started a business will confess that had they known about all the time, skills, and frustrations involved in starting and managing a business, they would never have done it. Even the people who are glad they started their own businesses will tell you it is not always a glamorous way of spending one's time and money. Numerous aspects of starting and managing a business are time consuming, repetitive, and mundane.

Nevertheless, starting your own business offers you the opportunity to experience things that are not otherwise available by working for someone else. If you know yourself, understand the nature of the marketplace, and possess the numerous skills necessary to start and manage a new business, then you should be in a position to beat the odds. You may also find it personally and financially rewarding.

As a first-timer, you are contemplating embarking on a journey many people think about but few people do much about. When you start your first business, to paraphrase the prelude to *Star Trek*, you are about to "boldly go where you have not gone before."

This guide is written for the "first timer"—the person who has limited business education and experience and wants to start his or her own business. It is intended to provide an entrepreneurial "blueprint" for starting a successful new venture. This book cannot guarantee success, but it does offer numerous ideas and insights which will increase your chances for beating the odds.

This book is not intended to encourage or discourage you from starting a new business. Instead, it is designed to help you size up your own strengths and limitations as well as have you look before you leap. Some readers will realize they are not willing to take the risk or they lack key skills. It is better to learn this now rather than after the business is started.

Other readers may find they have the confidence and competence but they need to rethink their business idea. Starting a business is like riding a horse. You may be a capable rider, but if your horse is weak, you will not go very far. The same applies to starting a business. New business success requires knowing what you are doing and capitalizing on a good opportunity. You may be ready, but market conditions also must be right. Be patient and don't be discouraged. This book will help you identify emerging opportunities.

A few readers may find they are ready and the marketplace is ripe with opportunities to harvest. If you are in this group, I wish you the best and offer you two pieces of advice. Fasten your seat belt and keep your copy of this book close by because you are about to embark on what may be a journey of a lifetime.

1
Creating a New Business

The United States may be characterized as a land of opportunity. One particular area of opportunity is the freedom to go into business for yourself. The free-enterprise system means people have the freedom to try to succeed. This freedom also involves the risk of failure.

The following material is designed to provide information and guidance about what people need to do in exercising their freedom to go into business and what people can do to reduce the likelihood of business failure. By no means does this "blueprint" presume to cover all the material available on the subject or to guarantee success. Instead, it is intended to provide a set of guidelines for people who are thinking about starting a business.

Starting your own business includes opportunities as well as risks. Profits have been defined as the reward for taking risks. The benefits of having your own business are twofold. First, considerable personal wealth can be generated from a well-managed business—even a one-person business. Second, and oftentimes the most satisfying aspect of running your own business, is the feeling of freedom associated with "being your own boss," making your own decisions, and building a business from scratch.

However, by choosing not to be an employee for someone else, you lose the security of a regular paycheck, a predictable work schedule, fringe benefits, paid vacations, and a retirement plan. Accordingly, having your own business involves risking your property, your health, and your pride. Each individual who is considering becoming his or her own boss should remember the old adage, "Nothing ventured, nothing gained...but also nothing lost."

Guidelines for Starting and Managing a Business

If there is one word that best describes the type of person who starts his or her own business, then it would have to be "optimistic." Yet even with this optimism, it is a cold and hard fact that more than half of the 700,000 businesses started this year will not be around three years from now. Only 20 percent of the businesses started this year will be around in 10 years. Half of the survivors will be producing only a marginal profit. The process of starting a business involves answering numerous questions. The first two questions to be answered are, "Do I have what it takes to be successful?" and "Am I starting a business where a real and lasting opportunity exists?"

Do You Have What It Takes to Successfully Start and Manage a New Business?

When the owners of businesses that failed are asked what contributed to their demise, they tend to say too much competition, high interest rates, government regulations, inflation, recession, and numerous other factors. Let's set the record straight. These factors may have contributed to their problems, but "mismanagement" is the primary reason for most business failures.

According to a study by Dun and Bradstreet, the lack of managerial experience and knowledge accounted for nearly 90 percent of all business failures. In most cases, the small business owner:

1. Entered a market that was already crowded with competition.
2. Did not offer exactly what people wanted to buy.
3. Failed to make the appropriate changes in business operations to meet a changing marketplace.
4. Lacked sufficient knowledge about that type of business in legal, financial, purchasing, accounting, employee relations, or marketing matters. This lack of knowledge will result in the inability to come up with the right answers when faced with pressing business decisions.

This is one of the reasons why franchises have been popular. Most franchisers screen people for business knowledge and experience. Some franchises also offer extensive training programs, ongoing management assistance, and a systematic rather than trial-and-error approach to running a business. For a fee, most franchises increase the probability of being successful. While success may not be guaranteed, their track record for success is considerably higher than the first-time independent business start-up.* Nearly four out of five franchisees succeed. Four out of five independent businesses fail within 10 years.

Yet with all the hazards and pitfalls, the dream of having your own business can be realized. Whether it is an independent business or a franchise, if you know what to do, how to do it, and when to do it, then you should be able to beat the odds.

Don't Be One of the Losers

In spite of differences in age, ethnic background, religious beliefs, and gender, most of the people who are successful in a small business have a lot in common. First, they were prepared to start their businesses. They usually had experience in that or a similar type of business. Anyone who is thinking of starting a business should get a job in that type of business first. There is no substitute for experience in small business. Experience offers insight into the nature of products, services, customer needs, employees, suppliers, seasonality, and so on. The high failure rate for new businesses in their first few years indicates that there is little room for mistakes. The average business makes only 4 cents profit per dollar of sales before taxes. The competitive world of business shows little mercy for the trial-and-error approach used by novices. Experience reduces some of the surprises first-timers encounter and enables them to anticipate most problems and prevent them. Experience as an employee, however, is not the same as "managing" that type of business. Obviously, managerial experience in that type of business will enhance your chances for success.

Experience may help, but education and formal training also are important. Just because you have done it before is no guarantee that you were doing it right or that it was the best way. Education and formal training in the "technical" fields of business, particularly accounting, finance, marketing, and law are essential in today's competitive times.

*This is not to be interpreted as a blanket endorsement of all franchises. Please consult with an attorney and an accountant when considering any franchise...or for that matter, when starting or buying any business. Franchises will be discussed in Chapter 11.

Your business will only be as good as the decisions you make. If you do not understand the uniqueness of the situation and do not possess state-of-the-art knowledge about how to identify opportunities and solve various types of problems, you are destined to fail. Education and experience will not guarantee success, but they will reduce the trial-and-error approach to managing that is the primary reason so many businesses fail.

The prospective business manager must also guard against adopting the attitude, "I'll just call my accountant or attorney and ask what I should do." At first glance, this seems like a logical attitude. To be successful, however, a manager needs to have a good working knowledge of every aspect of managing a small business. This isn't to say you shouldn't consult professional advisors on related matters. You *should* consult with them on technical matters. Moreover, you should consult with these professionals early in decision processes rather than after the fact. You will never know all the answers, but it is important that you know the questions that will need to be answered and where to get advice.

A small business is like a forest. If you do not have a good understanding of each tree (accounting, marketing, employee relations, etc.) and how the trees are interrelated, there is little likelihood that you will have the depth and breadth of knowledge necessary to make the right decisions. For example, managers of troubled businesses frequently cite "working capital" as a problem. In layperson terms, this means their expenses are greater than sales or that cash receipts and disbursements are not synchronized. They do not have enough cash to pay their rent, to replace their inventory, to meet their payroll, and so forth.

Working capital problems are actually multifaceted. Generally, managers will need to find ways to increase sales, reduce expenses, collect outstanding receivables, lower the amount of money tied up in inventory, and improve a dozen other areas. Few things exist in a vacuum in operating a business. The manager of a small business needs to be a good generalist and have specialists (possibly a partner or other employees) in the business or available to the business who can supplement the manager's knowledge.

Successful entrepreneurs exhibit eight qualities that separate them from most people:

1. They Are Opportunity Seekers. They live by the entrepreneurs' creed: "Within every problem lies a disguised opportunity." They are always looking for areas where people aren't having their needs met at all or well enough. They know there are an infinite number of opportunities in the marketplace. They recognize that more people working outside their homes will increase the demand for labor and time-saving appliances. They know that professional, two-income couples often prefer to write a check to have someone else paint their houses, cut their lawns, and do their errands. They are aware that people will be more concerned with their health, will look for ways to keep fit, and will prefer health-related foods. Accordingly, most entrepreneurs are frustrated because they know their lives are too short to harvest all the opportunities that exist today and that are destined to emerge in the years ahead.

2. They Are Future-Oriented. They have a vision of what is possible and are willing to invest their time and money in transforming their ideas into business ventures. They subscribe to Alan Kay's philosophy, "The best way to predict the future is to invent it." They don't live in the past nor will you hear them say, "In my day, we used to walk five miles through the snow to get to school." Just because something has not been done before does not mean that it cannot be done. They are in tune with the present and actively involved in monitoring trends that may reveal opportunities that are just over the horizon. They think at least three to five years ahead and are prepared to make short-term sacrifices to capitalize on long-term opportunities. They resist the temptation to pursue fads and are not seduced by get-rich-quick schemes. They know that as people live longer and enjoy better health than past generations, they will travel more and seek avenues for using their time more constructively. The "graying" of our population will create new opportunities for businesses that tailor their offerings to an aging population. The rising standard of living throughout the developing countries will also provide a myriad of opportunities for people who are prepared to create businesses to meet emerging needs. Entrepreneurs are prepared, as the prelude to *Star Trek* goes: "To boldly go where no man has gone before." They recognize that the first firm to enter an emerging market often establishes a formidable competitive position.

3. They Are Committed to Being the Best. They have contempt for the status quo. They know that the last eight words of a dying business are: "But that's the way we've always done it." They are always looking for new ways to do things and new things to do. They recognize that in a changing market what worked well yesterday will not work as well today, will be inappropriate tomorrow, and will be obsolete the day after. They are good learners and listeners; they know that running a business is a continuous process of learning, experimenting, and changing. They know that excellence does not come from hitting an occasional home run, it comes from hitting singles on a regular basis. They know that people who try to hit home runs frequently strike out. Success comes from doing almost everything well rather than just a few things in an exceptional fashion. As Tom Smith, president of Food Lion put it, "We don't try to be l000 percent better on a few things, we try to be at least 1 percent better than our competition on 1000 things." They also know that you will not succeed by imitating your competitors. You have to be better...and to be better you must have the courage, ability, and commitment to be different. They are willing to be the first business to have a 24-hour, seven-days-a-week toll-free ordering number, the first to deliver the product or service to customers, the first to install a drive-in window, the first to have the confidence to offer a satisfaction guaranteed, no-questions-asked full refund return policy.

4. They Are Market-Driven and Customer-Oriented.   They know that you are successful only to the extent that you are able to create and maintain customers for a profit. To paraphrase Stew Leonard, founder of Leonard's Dairy, "Customers don't come into my store and ask, 'What can I do for Stew Leonard today?' We must be constantly asking, 'What can we do for our customers?' " They know that businesses need to modify their approaches to fit the market, rather than try to change the market to fit what the owner wants to offer. They know their customers are the lifeblood of their businesses. They frequently ask their customers what they are looking for and how the business can be improved to meet their needs. Everyone in the business recognizes that customers actually provide the payroll, not the owner. They know that they are not in the business of selling goods or services; they are in the business of providing satisfaction. They view themselves as customer problem solvers and treat each customer as if the business's future is in his or her hands.

5. They Value Their Employees.   They recognize that a business will only be as good as its employees. They know that dedicated employees may be one of the business's greatest competitive advantages. They also know that the quality of customer relations is directly related to the quality of employee relations.

Successful entrepreneurs are honest in their dealings with all people, particularly their employees. Accordingly, they set the right example for their employees and try to involve them when making various decisions. Employees are encouraged to learn various activities so the business will not be dependent on only one person. Too many small businesses fail because the owner or manager made all the decisions and failed to develop a successor. If you are a perfectionist, it is unlikely you will delegate decisions or develop your people. The desire to be your own boss may be strong, but don't let it hurt your business.

Some small business owners actually drive away good employees because their employees are not offered a promising future or the opportunity to try their ideas. If you want to enjoy the benefits of having your own business such as having a flexible schedule and having a business that is capable of growing and sustaining good profits, then you will have to learn to delegate key decisions to your employees. If you are the type of person who needs to control everything and make every decision, then you are going to run yourself ragged and restrict the growth of your business. If you spend all your time "running the business," then you will not have the time to keep pace with the changes taking place in the marketplace or to develop innovative ways to create and maintain customers for a profit.

If you insist on making all the decisions because you feel no one can manage the business while you are gone, then you will be reluctant to take vacations or even an occasional day off. Small business owners need to recognize that no one has a monopoly on having all the right answers. Mark Shepherd, as chairman of Texas Instruments, once said, "Each employee needs to be viewed as a source of ideas, not just another pair of hands." If you want your business to grow, you must create an environment that encourages your people to contribute and grow. In short, your style of management may be one of the reasons your business does not grow. Another point worth noting is that a constrained employee today may quit and become your most formidable competitor tomorrow.

6. They Are Realistic. They know the difference between a dream and a solid business opportunity. They do know that wishful thinking will not cut it in the competitive marketplace. A new venture cannot be launched without a solid business plan. As Crawford H. Greenewalt of DuPont once noted, "If you fail to plan, you are planning to fail." They know that there are a lot of similarities between being a parent and starting a business. It is a lot easier to conceive of a business than to keep it going. They know that starting a business is not something to be taken lightly. It is not like starting a new hobby or going on a diet. It is not something that can be turned on and off like a light switch.

They look before they leap. They don't test the depth of a stream by jumping in with both feet. They do their homework, gather the data, plan their work, and then work their plan. They also know that life is full of surprises. They also know that there are no time-outs where you can stop the world so you can get your act together. They know that to succeed in the long haul, you're going to have to be the best. They also know lasting success comes from good management, not good luck.

They acknowledge that the business world is not a perfect place and that people don't always play by the rules. They realize that their competitors' ads and salespeople may not be truthful in their promotional claims. They know employees will not always show up for work and that when they do, they may help themselves to their employer's inventory and supplies. They have also learned that suppliers will not always honor their promises. They know that when suppliers say it was shipped yesterday, it probably wasn't and that if it was, it probably wasn't exactly what they ordered. They also know that if you create a better mousetrap, the world may not beat a path to your door. Instead, the few people who slowly trickle into your store may inform you that another business just opened down the street...and that it is offering your new product or service at one-half your price! Successful entrepreneurs realize there are no free lunches and no guarantees for success. There is only one way to make a profit in the game of business: you have to do it the old-fashioned way—you have to earn it.

7. They Are Tolerant of the Tedium.   They know that being an entrepreneur is not that glamorous. They know life is full of compromises. It also involves mundane activities and thankless tasks. Starting a business involves blood, sweat, and tears. Most people believe starting a business is a labor of love. Most entrepreneurs are quick to acknowledge that the labor often exceeds the love.

The story of the woman who was being interviewed to be a housekeeper who said, "I won't do windows" has direct application to starting a business. When you start a business, you must be prepared to do whatever is necessary. You may be excited about going off on buying trips and putting together creative sales promotions, but you'll also have to keep track of all payroll-related expenses, monitor inventory levels, and deal with employee problems and anything else that comes up. There will be many days when you feel as if you spent the whole day plugging holes in the dike with your thumbs.

They recognize that life is also a matter of compromise. You may want to have your cake and eat it too, but you are going to have to shop for the ingredients, toil in the kitchen making it, and spend time cleaning up. They know that the excitement associated with the honeymoon of starting a business can quickly become 60- to 80-hour workweeks. This means that your family and friends may have to be put on hold on a regular basis and that unexpected business situations will force you to cancel personal plans more often than you would like. As one entrepreneur once observed, "Being your own boss may eventually have its benefits, but in the early years it also means packing your own lunch. You will not be able to go to lunch until you hire your first employee because until then, no one would be there to answer the phone if you were to go out to lunch."

8. They Are Resilient. They know that business success is not a 100-meter sprint; it is a marathon. There are few overnight successes. As someone noted, "It may take two years to know if your business is a lemon and seven years to know if it's a pearl." Success is not just the result of having a great idea or identifying a "gap" in the marketplace; it takes patience and persistence. It means handling the conflict, compromises, and competition. It means being driven from within because there will be times when no one is going to be there to pat you on the back to say, "Hang in there, things will get better."

Starting and managing a business is not smooth sailing. It is more like canoeing through rapids. You are never in total control, you cannot foresee everything that is around the bend, and there are going to be times when you have to improvise just to keep afloat. You must have what is called "a tolerance for the turbulence." As Fred Murphy put it, "If sailing on a big and placid lake is your style, go to work for a large corporation, but if white-water canoeing is to your liking, try a small company."

They know decisions must be made even though they won't have all the information they want and that the person who procrastinates will be passed by. They know that they must have the courage of their convictions and that they will also have to listen, to learn, and to be flexible. They know they will have to make judgment calls and that there is no way to eliminate risk.

They also know that in business they will need to have the strength to hang in there when things get tough. They know there are more losers than winners. They will be the first to admit that creating a viable business is a constant challenge and a perpetual juggling act. To succeed takes more than being street smart, it also takes an almost inexhaustible supply of energy.

Most entrepreneurs experience one or two failures before they experience their first success. Most successful entrepreneurs have demonstrated the ability to take a punch, pick themselves up, dust themselves off, learn from their experiences, and re-energize themselves in a better way. Experience shows that what you do when things get tough and how you handle failure may have a lot to do with whether you will succeed.

Conclusion: Starting a Business Is Survival of the Fittest

This chapter has had one simple message, "Starting a business is not a casual undertaking." The deck is stacked against you. If you are going to accept the challenge, then you must do everything you can to improve your chances for success. You will need to have: (1) a solid business opportunity, (2) the necessary skills and abilities, (3) the right approach to doing business, and (4) sufficient funds to start and operate the business until it can stand on its own.

This chapter has helped identify some of the personal qualities that may give you an edge in the competitive arena. If you have not been discouraged, then you may find it worthwhile to take the following "Entrepreneurial Qualities Self-Test."

You may not have the answers for the first five questions, but you need to give these questions serious thought. You may not get the highest ratings on all "eight entrepreneurial qualities"; even the most successful entrepreneurs have certain weaknesses. If you have a low score on most of the eight qualities, then you should think twice about starting a business. The process of starting a business and keeping it going is not the job for someone who prefers to be a "caretaker." Entrepreneurs are people who enjoy the opportunity to change the world around them. If you want to simplify your life and play it safe, then work for someone else...don't consider being an entrepreneur. As André Maurois noted, "Business is a combination of war and sport." You may not have the goal of being in the Inc. 500 in the next 5 years and in the Fortune 500 within 10 years, but you will need to have certain qualities if you are to succeed in the competitive arena.

Entrepreneurial Qualities Self-Test: Part 1

1. Why am I going into business? (For the money, the freedom, the challenge, for employment for myself and family?)

    Answer:_____

2. What is the minimum annual salary I would accept in return for quitting my job and starting a business?

    Answer: $_____ per year.

3. What is the amount of time I am willing to commit to starting and managing a business?

Answer: The maximum number of hours per week _____.
The minimum number of hours per week _____.

4. What is the maximum amount of risk of business failure I am willing to accept? (One chance in 10, or 10 percent; 3 chances in 10, or 30 percent; etc.)

    Answer: I am willing to accept a _____ chance in 10, or a _____ percent chance of failure.

5. How long do you plan to have the business?

    Answer: I expect to be involved in the business as its owner for at least _____ years.

6. How do I rate on the eight entrepreneurial qualities?

	Low		Medium		High
a. I am an opportunity seeker.	1	2	3	4	5

    If you do not already have at least two opportunities that have merit, then give yourself one point. If you are the type of person who is constantly identifying opportunities in numerous areas, then give yourself five points.

    b. I am future-oriented.   1   2   3   4   5

    If you are always reading about the past, committed to maintaining traditions, and frequently reminisce about the "good old days," then give yourself one point. If you are fascinated with technological change and space exploration, are one of the first people to try new products, and monitor global sociopolitical trends, then give yourself five points.

    c. I am committed to being the best.   1   2   3   4   5

    If you have a habit of just doing enough to get by and are usually late (even if it is only by five minutes) for social and professional events, then give yourself one point. If you are the type of person who strives to be the best in everything you pursue, who takes pleasure in going beyond the call of duty, who is willing to learn new things, and who believes there is always a better way, then give yourself five points.

    d. I am market-driven and customer-oriented.

    1   2   3   4   5

    If you don't like meeting other people and believe that you always know what is best, then give yourself one point. If you enjoy helping other people, even strangers, and are always open to other people's ideas for how things (including yourself) can be improved, then give yourself five points.

	Low		Medium		High

e. I value employees.   1   2   3   4   5

If you prefer to work alone, believe that if you want the job done right you're going to have to do it yourself, have been divorced at least once, and feel people would have to be gluttons for punishment if they want to have children today, then give yourself one point. If you believe work can be a rewarding experience, that people will be responsible if you give them responsibility, and that your best employees should have the opportunity to become partners or buy stock in your business, then give yourself five points.

f. I am realistic.   1   2   3   4   5

If you believe that if you have faith, things will work out for the best, that good intentions will always prevail, and that hard work is all that it takes to succeed, then give yourself one point. If you believe that life is what you make it, the deck is stacked against a new business, and that most business decisions are judgment calls, then give yourself five points.

g. I am tolerant of the tedium.   1   2   3   4   5

If you won't do your own tax preparation, haven't waxed your car yourself in the last two years, and haven't flossed your teeth since your last dental appointment, then give yourself one point. If you don't procrastinate doing tedious, time-consuming tasks like those mentioned, then give yourself five points.

h. I am resilient.   1   2   3   4   5

If you are hesitant to try something you have never done before, are not willing to speak in public, and mope around after you have failed at something, then give yourself one point. If you look forward to new challenges and traveling to foreign lands; thrive on unstructured, ambiguous, uncertain situations; and bounce back with renewed vigor after experiencing a setback, then give yourself five points.

Entrepreneurial Qualities
Self-Test: Part 1 Score Sheet

How do I rate on the eight entrepreneurial qualities?

Quality	Low		Medium		High
1. Opportunity seeker	1	2	3	4	5
2. Future-oriented	1	2	3	4	5
3. Committed to being the best	1	2	3	4	5
4. Market-driven and customer-oriented	1	2	3	4	5
5. Value employees	1	2	3	4	5
6. Realistic	1	2	3	4	5
7. Tolerant of the tedium	1	2	3	4	5
8. Resilient	1	2	3	4	5
Total points		= _____			

Scoring Breakdown

1. If your total score is *less than 20 points*, then get a safe job in a large organization or try to win the lottery so you don't need to work.

2. If your total score is *between 20 and 25 points*, then take a look at your attitudes and see if you can adopt a more entrepreneurial approach to life.

3. If your total score is *more than 25 points*, then you have some of the entrepreneurial qualities. This is no guarantee for success, but it means that you can proceed to the next chapter.

2
Identifying New Business Opportunities

An Opportunity Can Be Found Within Every Problem

If you are satisfied that you have the personal qualities needed to start a new business, then the next question is, "What type of business should I start?" The greatest mistake people make when starting a new business is that they try to sell products they like. People who like reading want to start bookstores. People who like animals want to start pet shops. People who like to dine out or to cook want to start restaurants. This may be human nature, but it is a backwards approach to starting a business.

The first law of marketing is "You need to offer what people want to buy, not what you want to sell." Customers do not buy what you like, they buy what they want.

The first step in determining what type of business to start is to do market research or to "listen to the market." Too many people start a "business in search of customers." This tends to be an exercise in futility. By listening to the market, we can find "customers in search of a business."

Creating Customers

Customers in search of a business are people who are not having their particular needs and wants met at all or well enough. Think about your own purchasing behavior. If existing businesses do not offer exactly what you want, then you either do not buy at all or you are still searching for the business that will give you what you are looking for.

Market research merely tries to identify where people's needs are not being met, how many people are in that category, what exactly they are looking for, how much they are willing to pay, how you can get in touch with them, and what is the best way to get what they want to them. In the United States, there are over 240 million people. Few people are getting exactly what they want. Therefore, millions of customers are in search of a business.

When customers finally find a business that offers what they want, they tend to thank the manager for taking their money. They also tell their friends, neighbors, and colleagues about that business. How's that for free advertising? The more you offer what people want to buy, the less they are affected by your competitors' advertisements, price cutting, or location. A high degree of customer loyalty to a business is one of the factors that separates the winners from the losers.

Anyone thinking of starting a new business must heed the saying: "The purpose of a business is to create and maintain customers for a profit." Almost every new business starts without the benefit of having any customers. Getting customers is only half the battle. Keeping them is the other half.

Quite a few businesses have failed because their managers saw themselves as "selling products and services." Successful managers know that businesses only make a profit when they "provide satisfaction." Numerous large firms have based their advertising programs on the "marketing concept" of listening to the market and tailoring their offerings to meet the needs of specific groups of customers. Toyota's slogan has been, "You asked for it, you got it!" Penney's slogan at one time was, "At Penney's we know what you're looking for!" Burger King is known for its "Have it your way!" slogan. When the other hamburger franchises were out of tune with a number of people's preferences, Wendy's initiated its "Where's the beef?" ad campaign.

When you offer what people want, at a price that is fair, in a reasonably convenient manner, then you are one step closer to "creating a customer." You may be able to "sell" something you stock to some people, but you have not created customers unless they want to come back and have talked favorably about your business to people they know. When you are trying to decide what to offer, remember the saying, "Successful businesses offer goods and services that don't come back, and they offer them to people who do!"

Maintaining Customers

To "maintain" customers, you need to stay in tune with them and change your business to meet their changing needs and expectations. This is a never-ending process. Even the most successful businesses lose customers on a regular basis. A rule of thumb is that the average business loses one-third of its customers each year. Customers move away, switch to one of the competitors whose offering is more consistent with their desires, lose their need for such a product or service, or die. As you can see, even established businesses need to consistently listen to the market for customers in search of a business as well as change their operations to keep in tune with their existing customers.

New businesses and businesses that want to grow have to work even harder to establish or expand their customer base. Managers who do not listen to the market or who take their customers for granted are destined to fail. If you conduct market research on an ongoing basis, treat each customer as if that person is your business's only customer, and fine-tune your business to what the market wants; then you will increase the likelihood of being successful. Remember, the marketplace is like the tide. Instead of trying to change it, concentrate your attention on where it is and where it is heading. If you can sense upcoming changes and offer the market what it wants, the way it wants it, and when it wants it, you may find owning a business to be a mentally and financially rewarding endeavor.

Are There Any Opportunities Left for New Businesses?

Quite a few people are skeptical about whether someone can start a new business in a world that appears to be dominated by large firms. The perennial questions remain, "Can a new David compete in a world of Goliaths?" and "Do new businesses only get big businesses' table scraps?" Nearly every large firm was once a new small business that was able to establish itself against larger competitors. So the answer is a resounding, "Yes...they can compete." Yet the most likely way to succeed is not to compete against bigger firms.

Most small businesses should avoid competing head-to-head with larger, established businesses. This is particularly true when it comes to price competition and the breadth and depth of product selection. Most large firms enjoy "economies of scale." They can buy their goods in larger quantities and qualify for quantity discounts. If they are manufacturers, they may be able to produce the product at a lower unit cost. Larger firms are usually able to carry a broader selection of products than smaller businesses. For example, large retail stores may carry numerous brands (product breadth) and a number of models (product depth) in their effort to attract a large number and variety of customers. Some "mega" stores try to offer one-stop shopping by having something for everyone.

Your new small business may have a better chance to succeed if you do not try to compete with larger firms on the same basis. Instead, you should try to identify what consumers want but the larger firms do not offer at all or well enough. In certain cases, bigger does not guarantee being better. Almost all large businesses have weaknesses; it is impossible to be everything for everybody.

Big businesses are built on compromise. They need to generate a high volume of business to cover the investment associated with the large-scale operations needed to serve large markets and provide economies of scale. Economies of scale are only possible when you can serve mass markets or large groups of consumers with similar interests. Sears, Wal-Mart, K-mart, and most large retailers use this strategy. Ironically, their attempt to keep their costs down so they can appeal to consumers via lower prices has created opportunities for smaller businesses. As already noted, most attempts by small retail businesses to compete by price alone may be futile. The probability for success may be much higher if they are willing to compete in other ways where big businesses may not be able to be as competitive in creating and maintaining customers for a profit. Your small business's competitive advantage may rest with your ability to tailor your offering to small groups of consumers...to meet a few people's needs very well rather than a lot of people's needs in a lukewarm manner.

The following example illustrates how a new business may be able to attract customers. Mary Smith graduated with a degree in agricultural sciences 10 years ago from Midwestern State University. Since that time, she has been working for the county agricultural extension service in Decatur, Illinois. The idea of having her own business has been on her mind for the last few years. Mary has been thinking about starting a lawn and garden center. Her whole life has revolved around helping people grow plants.

A few months ago, Mary recognized that it would be worthwhile to ask Susan Williams out to lunch. Susan was one of Mary's sorority sisters at Midwestern State University. Susan is now a business consultant with a regional accounting firm. Mary conveyed her interest in starting a lawn and garden center and her desire to open it in her hometown. Susan informed Mary that she had already violated the first two business commandments: (1) "Thou shall not start a business just because you like the products" and (2) "Thou shall not open a business in a geographic area just because you would like to live there." Susan indicated there may be better business opportunities and better locations. However, Mary insisted that her mind was made up and that she was prepared to accept the risk.

Their conversation then shifted to what Mary could do to increase her chances of success. One of Mary's first concerns involved how she would be able to compete against some of the larger department and discount stores in her hometown. Mary had already checked around and learned that the garden shop at one of the large stores offered a 50-pound bag of lime for $1.39. Mary found this disturbing because the suppliers of the same brand of lime told her the price to small retailers is $1.40 per bag. Mary would have to pay more for a bag than what her large competitors were selling it for!

The suppliers suggested a retail price that would be a 40 percent markup on cost. That meant that Mary would be selling the same 50-pound bag of lime for $1.96 that the discount store was selling for $1.39. Mary would have a significant price disadvantage. To make matters worse, the price differential on many of the products she planned to carry was not that different from that of the bags of lime. Some suppliers even indicated that she was too small for them to supply her. Mary wondered how she would be able to create and maintain customers for a profit if she had this price differential and might not even be able to carry some of the most popular brands. In spite of her frustration, Mary believed there was a market. If she could come up with ways to beat the competition, then she would continue investigating the possibility of starting a garden center.

Susan used the lime example to illustrate how a small business may be able to establish a competitive advantage. She identified the following possibilities:

1. Identify a target market (group of consumers) who will be doing a lot of landscaping and who are not located within a 10-minute drive of the larger department-discount stores. Many consumers are not willing to drive all the way across town to save a few cents. This is particularly true for consumers who have high incomes and who value their free time.

2. Offer bags of lime in different sizes. Who says everyone wants a 50-pound bag? Some people won't be able to lift a 50-pound bag. Other people won't want to store what they don't use. Mary may be able to carry 10-pound bags...or better yet, to sell it by the pound. That way she will be able to offer the quantity of lime the customers want to buy and use rather than some standardized size that is convenient for the firm packaging the lime.

3. Mary may provide a soil analysis service for her customers for free or at a minimal charge. Mary will be able to determine if customers need lime and how much will be needed.

4. Mary could offer a delivery service for purchases over $10. Most department-discount stores do not deliver.

5. Mary could rent lime spreaders for a nominal rate. After all, how many consumers want to buy a $20 to $30 spreader to be used once a year?

6. One of her employees could spread the lime for a fee.

7. There are many other ways that Mary could offer her customers far more than a bag of lime. The ultimate case would be for her customers to call her garden center and have one of her employees: (1) come out to do a soil sample, (2) determine the amount of lime needed, (3) apply the lime periodically, (4) and have it charged to the customers' credit cards. This service "package" would run between $30 and $50 per half-acre yard. This service could be available as an annual contract for individual residences and institutions. Mary could offer a similar service for weed-killing fertilizer in the spring, greening fertilizer in August, and rye grass in October. Mary could also offer a flower planting service throughout the year.

The more that Mary can give select groups of customers exactly what they want, the less that the price differential for the bag of lime will affect her business. By offering her customers a "have it your way" approach to doing business, she may be able to create and maintain customers for a profit. The discount store may have an average lime-related sale of less than $2; Mary may be able to generate an average lime-related sale of $20 by providing the additional services.

It is safe to say that not all of Mary's customers would be interested in these services. This is why large stores would not consider offering these services. Large discount stores are geared to consumers who tend to be price-sensitive and willing to do the work themselves. However,

Mary may find a segment of people who will be delighted to substitute their money for their time and effort.

Mary will have a better chance of being successful if she adopts the "swiss cheese" approach. Every marketplace has "holes" of opportunity for small businesses. These holes represent gaps in the market where big businesses cannot or choose not to go. Big businesses tend to be a bit choosy; they tend to leave quite a few table scraps lying around. Big businesses will not locate in every small town, they cannot meet everyone's unique needs, they do not change very quickly, and they are not very flexible. For example, small clothing boutiques exist because large department stores tend to offer products that will appeal to most people. Boutiques are designed to offer people with money and particular tastes a select line of products and services that cannot be found at the larger stores. Discriminating buyers do not want to buy something right off the rack that can be found at most stores; they want things that are unique.

There are at least two other areas of opportunity for new businesses. Opportunities exist for new businesses to serve or supply larger businesses. Most large businesses rely on smaller businesses to supply them with products and services. Larger firms frequently look to employment agencies, maintenance businesses, trucking firms, and numerous other businesses as an alternative to doing these functions for themselves. This trend is expected to continue in the future.

The trend toward a service economy is expected to continue in the twenty-first century. This represents a particularly attractive area of opportunity for new businesses. Service businesses usually require less money to start on a small scale. Due to limited economies of scale, larger businesses may not have a cost advantage. The relative competitive strength for smaller businesses is evident in the lawn and garden center example. At first glance, it appeared that Mary was selling products such as lime, fertilizer, and plants. However, a closer look reveals that Mary's strength would be in the services she offered.

Yes, There Are Opportunities!

The moral to this chapter is that if you can offer products that people want but cannot find at existing businesses, then you may be able to create and maintain customers for a profit. The greatest opportunity, however, may be in the area of services. If you can provide goods and services in a quicker, more convenient, less expensive, or higher quality manner, then you may have an edge in the competitive arena. The bottom line is that you should start with a real opportunity, not just a personal desire; you should start with the current going in your favor. Mary was reducing her chances for success because she selected her business before she determined if it was a viable opportunity. The best way to start a business is to spend considerable time analyzing the market for opportunities.

What Kind of Business Should I Start?

The following six-step process can be used when deciding what type of business to start:

Step 1: Listing Problems in the Marketplace

Step 2: Identifying Corresponding Business Opportunities

Step 3: Determining the Needed Capabilities and Resources

Step 4: Projecting the Financial Dimensions

Step 5: Ranking the Opportunities in Terms of Personal Preferences, Financial Worthiness, and Perceived Risk

Step 6: Selecting the Business Opportunity to Pursue

Only after you have identified the opportunities, evaluated your capabilities, and determined the potential profitability for each business venture will you be in a position to consider starting your own business.

Step 1: Listing Problems in the Marketplace

The first step in starting a new venture begins with listening to the marketplace. The prospective entrepreneur needs to generate a list of areas where people's needs are not being met well enough or at all. It is particularly important that you do not restrict yourself to one particular type of product, service, or geographic area. You should keep an open mind and a broad perceptual field.

It has been said that a decision will only be as good as the best alternative. This also applies to starting a new venture. Your business will never be any better than the strength of the market need. This situation is similar to a horse race. Someone once observed that no jockey ever carried the horse across the finish line. The same applies to starting a business. Regardless of how astute you may be in business (as a rider), if the market (the horse) isn't there to support you, you're not going to go very far.

Attention needs to be directed to generating a sizeable list of market problems. The quantity of problems is more important than their respective quality at this time. Subsequent steps will look at the relative quality of each problem.

The "Market Gap" Approach to Identifying Problems.   Richard M. White, Jr., offers an interesting approach for identifying problems or "gaps" in the marketplace in his book, *The Entrepreneur's Manual* (Clifton Book Company, 1977). According to White, you can find opportunities in almost any aspect of life. He uses the example of looking at problems encountered by adults. Through a sequence of questions, White divides adult life into work vs. leisure. White then narrows his focus to the time of day when adults encounter problems. In this example, White concentrates his attention on problems people encounter "after work but before dinner on weekdays." White's list of problems includes: fatigue, heavy traffic, feet are tired and hot, clothes are rumpled and cling, the dog must be taken out to do its business, telephone solicitors are irritating, etc. White indicates that hundreds of problems are common just during the brief "leisure-adult workday-postwork-predinner" time interval. The same "market gap" analysis could be applied to other aspects of life including: (1) adults traveling with preschool-age children via airlines, (2) owners of powerboats over 20 feet long after the summer is over, or (3) college freshmen moving away from home for the first time.

Extra effort needs to be taken to avoid judging the relative merit of each problem. Step 1 is intended only to list problems in the marketplace. Step 2 is designed to ascertain whether business opportunities may be disguised within the list of problems.

Step 2: Identifying Corresponding Business Opportunities

Attention is now directed to whether each problem or gap can be transformed into a business opportunity. One of the interesting things about this step is that each problem or gap may foster numerous different business opportunities. People having idle time while in airports waiting for flights provides a good example. Opportunities to reduce the idle time could include: (l) a one-hour laundry service for the business traveler who is going from city to city and wants to travel light; (2) a "nap hotel" that provides a Pullman-type berth with an alarm that permits the traveler to nap with privacy for an hour or more; (3) a business services center providing fax and photocopying machines, computers, secretarial assistance, a message center, and even a private meeting room; or (4) a health club providing massage, hot tub, sauna, etc., to take the edge off traveling. One enterprising individual recently started a business to turn idle time into recreational time. He has rented a relatively small retail space in Denver's Stapleton Field. He offers a golf driving range that videotapes your swing and provides feedback on your drive.

Each problem area or gap needs to be "exploded" into various possible business opportunities. Step 2 calls for an open mind and mental dexterity. The questions, "Which business can I do?" and "Which ones will be profitable?" should be avoided at this time. Step 2 only deals with whether there may be ways to address the problems.

In the United States, not to mention other countries, there are millions of customers in search of businesses. Nearly every person in the marketplace has needs that are not being met at all or well enough. The people who started some of this nation's most successful businesses listened to the market. They knew, "Within every problem there may be a disguised opportunity." They knew that by identifying problems in the marketplace, they would find customers in search of a business. Big problems mean big opportunities. Businesses that have become household names were started by entrepreneurs who listened to the market. They heard people saying, "I wish there was a business that..." Then, they created businesses to offer what the market wanted.

Some of Today's Most Popular Businesses Were Yesterday's New Ventures. In the late 1960s, Perry Mendel kept hearing parents of young children expressing frustration over the lack of day-care facilities. He researched the existing state of day care in the south and found that most day-care operations were run as individual businesses. He also learned that many day-care facilities were being run out of people's homes. Existing day-care facilities were not conducive to providing day care for a large number of children. The locations may have been convenient for the owners of the day-care businesses, but they were not convenient for the parents of the children.

Perry Mendel's research indicated that most existing customers were still in search of a business. His study of trends also revealed that the market for day-care services would experience rapid growth for quite a few years. Industry trends indicated that nearly 50 percent of all women would be employed by 1980. He recognized that with more women working, especially women with preschool-age children, there would be a greater need for high-quality day-care service.

Perry Mendel believed a professionally managed day-care business could be set up to offer first-class service at locations that were on the way to and from work. By providing the latest toys and recreational facilities, including a swimming pool in warmer geographic areas, and offering nutritious meals at a price no higher than traditional mom-and-pop backyard day-care businesses, these centers could capture a significant part of the market. Mendel's Kinder-Care, Inc., has become the largest day-care business in the free world.

Kinder-Care, Inc., is not the only small business success story. Every large business started with a person who listened to the market and had the mental dexterity to identify the opportunities that were disguised as problems. Henry and Richard Bloch* listened to the market and heard people who were frustrated with having to prepare their tax returns each year. The Blochs recognized that millions of people did not know how to prepare their tax returns, wanted a second opinion so they could sleep at night, or wanted to reduce their tax obligation. They found people would be willing to pay a small fee if reliable tax preparation could be provided at convenient times and locations. The Blochs figured they would be very successful if they could capture even 1 percent of the market. H & R Block is now available coast to coast. Trade data indicates that H & R Block handles close to 10 percent of all individual tax returns in the United States.

In the 1950s, Anthony A. Martino sensed another problem experienced by millions of people at one time or another. He recognized that America had become a society of automobile owners. He also realized that automobiles frequently break down. Anthony Martino analyzed the various auto problems and the extent to which customers were still in search of a business. He knew he would be better off repairing cars rather than manufacturing them, because service businesses usually take far less capital to start and he would be facing less formidable competitors.

Anthony Martino listened to the market and found a "gap." Sooner or later, most cars need transmission repair or replacement. He heard the market saying people were unable to have their needs met well enough by the existing businesses. Auto dealers specialized in selling cars, and service stations specialized in selling gasoline. Few businesses specialized in transmission repair or replacement. Anthony Martino carefully analyzed customer needs as well as the nature and extent of competition. He then developed AAMCO Transmission Services. Martino chose AAMCO for a name because his business would appear near the beginning of the yellow pages and his initials are A. A. M.

In 1972, Anthony Martino realized that there must be other problems in the automobile industry that were business opportunities in disguise.

---

*Their last name is Bloch, but they chose to use the name Block for their business.

Again, he listened to the market. This time he found that cars have a bad habit of hitting other cars. Sooner or later, most people get into an accident that requires bodywork and repainting. Anthony Martino found few businesses specialized in this side of auto work. As with transmissions, customers were in search of a business. When he had to select a name for his business, he merely reversed his initials and started MAACO for Martino, Anthony A., Company. Over 5 million vehicles have been painted or repaired at MAACO centers.

Anthony Martino's effort to create new ventures for "customers in search of a business" appears to be endless. In 1981, he started SPARKS Tune-Up Centers. The one-price tune-up and oil and lube service is completed within 45 minutes and backed by a written warranty. He also has attempted to end the mystery surrounding tune-up shops by encouraging customers to enter the car bays and watch while the service technicians work on their vehicles. Today, there are over 150 centers in 26 states.

Kurt Ziebart was another person to see the almost unlimited opportunities created by the millions of automobiles. In the 1960s, he recognized the growing desire by people to keep their cars longer as a way to beat inflation contrasted with the inability of auto manufacturers to make car bodies that would last as long as the mechanical parts. He compared existing businesses with consumer needs. He found customers in search of a business. He developed Ziebart Rustproofing Centers. For less than 3 percent of the price of a new car and one day's time, his rustproofing process usually extended the life of a car by a couple of years. The cost-benefit ratio, convenient locations, and one-day service proved to be a formula for success. There are over 600 Ziebart outlets in the world.

Ray Kroc had been employed as a food service equipment salesperson. However, when the company he worked for refused to consider distribution of a new five-spindle mixer, which Kroc felt would increase his cup sales, he decided it was time to start his own business. He obtained the national marketing rights to the mixer and started his own company in 1939. While he was traveling in California he stopped in to see one of his customers to learn why they were buying so many mixers. When Ray Kroc saw the drive-in restaurant run by the McDonald brothers, he saw more than a place that sold a lot of hamburgers. He saw a concept that could be franchised from coast to coast. Ray Kroc recognized that California was a good barometer of changing tastes in America and the growing desire for convenience.

In 1947, Burton Baskin and Irv Robbins recognized that the population was interested in variety and that vanilla, strawberry, and chocolate ice cream no longer met the market's interest in different flavors. They started Baskin-Robbins 31 Flavors. Years later, they recognized that even though fast-food franchises were growing in popularity, they did not offer much in the way of desserts. Baskin and Robbins used what is called a "parasite" approach and located their franchises as close as possible to fast-food franchises. This marketing decision was beneficial because they did not have to do as much advertising. The need for investing in large parking lots was also reduced. Quite a few of their customers just walked over to Baskin-Robbins from the fast-food franchises. The Baskin-Robbins' formula for success appears to be working. There are over 3000 stores worldwide that sell ice cream to over one and a half million customers each day.

Some of Today's "Gaps" May Produce Tomorrow's Success Stories. The preceding examples reinforce the point that listening to the market can pay off. Thousands of new businesses will be started this year by people who find "gaps" in the market. Some of the start-ups are almost destined to succeed. Business magazines, including *Inc.*, *Entrepreneur*, and *In Business*, frequently provide examples of new start-ups where entrepreneurs found an area in the market where a specific group of consumers were not having their needs met at all or well enough. The following six businesses* illustrate that the entrepreneurial strategy of starting a business where "customers are in search of a business" may still be one of the best ways to identify opportunities for a new business.

1. *Aqua Vox, Inc.* Michael Benjamin recognized that one of the most frustrating aspects of scuba diving was the inability of scuba divers to communicate with one another while underwater. He has developed a device that sells for $100 that permits underwater communication. Michael's problem/opportunity/capability/profitability equation appears to be right on target; his firm's first-year sales exceeded $1 million.

2. *My Own Meals, Inc.* Mary Ann Jackson was able to turn a nighttime routine into a new business. She recognized that one of the cumbersome aspects of being a parent involves preparing a child's lunch for the next day. Her company was the first to market on a large scale packaged meals for kids aged two to eight. The entrees, which retail for less than $3, are pressure-cooked and vacuum-sealed in plastic pouches. Mary Ann expects sales to exceed $500,000 in her first year and to be profitable in the next year.

3. *Tweedies Optical, Inc.* Tweedy Prager encountered a problem finding appropriate eyeglasses for her three-year-old twins. She found

---

*These examples were from the November 1988 issue of *Venture* magazine.

most eyeglasses were merely downsized versions of adult frames. She started her business to market a line of "spiffy specks" eyeglass frames that are attractive and fun to wear. Her line of frames for kids from 4 to 8 years old was so well received that she is now developing a line of frames for children between 9 and 13 years old.

4. *Shark Products, Inc.* Dave Medrick demonstrated that not all new products need to be for high-technology markets. He found that beachgoers are frequently frustrated when their towels blow away in the wind. He developed 6-inch plastic stakes tipped with a clothespin-like device resembling a shark that keeps the towel anchored and clean. Dave expects to sell 200,000 sharks in his first year. Like most entrepreneurs, he does not want to leave any stone unturned. Dave is already developing a device to hold tablecloths to picnic tables.

5. *Abt Enterprises.* Nancy Abt came to the conclusion that there must be a better way to help people cool off in the heat of the summer. She developed and received a patent on her product, The Cool Advantage. Her new product holds blocks of foam that are soaked in salt water. When the blocks, which are in polyurethane insulating bags, are frozen, they are colder than regular ice. Her product comes with a cloth cover seamed with Velcro strips, which allows people to wear it while playing tennis or any other sport. Nancy is already looking at other target markets as additional potential customers for her product, particularly at anyone who may need heat or muscle relief, such as chefs or people who suffer from multiple sclerosis.

6. *Pacific Bio Systems, Inc.* Arthur Peterson and Francis Keery illustrate the concept that if you develop a product that is quicker and better, then you may be able to get consumers to switch to your new product. They recognized a problem experienced by medical personnel in every hospital. Their research revealed that it usually takes doctors 10 minutes to scrub their hands and arms before surgery. They developed an automatic handwashing machine called Stat Scrub. Doctors place their hands and forearms into "sleeves" that clean them in less than two minutes. Their machine also is better at eliminating bacteria than manual scrubbing. They project sales to be around $300,000 in their first year. Arthur and Francis are similar to Nancy Abt in that they are also looking for additional groups of consumers who may be in search of better and quicker ways to clean their hands and arms. They are looking at people who manufacture chemicals, pharmaceuticals, and computer components as potential target markets.

The preceding examples represent a fraction of the thousands of new product-service opportunities that exist today. They also illustrate two interesting points. First, listening to the market for customers in search of a business may be far more fruitful than trying to generate new business ideas from scratch. The "market needs first, product-service second" sequence is what separates the entrepreneur from the inventor. The best entrepreneurs begin by identifying unmet needs rather than product-service ideas. If the entrepreneur can identify an unmet need, in most instances, he or she can develop or contract with someone else to develop the product-service to meet the need.

Second, the preceding examples indicate that new business opportunities are not restricted to high-technology products. Most promising new business opportunities exist in improving everyday life for regular people. It is interesting to note that in the last few years, two of the fastest growing firms were SOAP'S and Visible Changes. SOAP'S combines a laundromat with a pub-cafe. The franchisers of SOAP'S recognized that most people who were using laundromats were in search of constructive ways to use their time between wash cycles. SOAP'S provided a food and beverage outlet for them. One person picked up on the idle time concept and started a laundromat with a beauty parlor. Now their customers can enhance their personal appearances and clean their clothes at the same time.

Visible Changes is an example of the benefits of providing a service in a better, quicker, less expensive, or more convenient manner. John and Maryanne McCormack observed that most salons are mom-and-pop operations. They located their Visible Changes salons in shopping malls and utilized professional management techniques to create and maintain customers. Their average outlet's revenue is nearly five times the revenue of the typical salon.

Another enterprising individual recognized that businesses are still searching for ways to advertise their products and services. This entrepreneur leased the inside of the doors for the bathroom stalls at airports. He then made money selling ads that he put on the doors.

Fred DeLuca also demonstrates that you don't need to have an MBA or a high-tech product to succeed. He is one of America's more recent success stories. After graduating from high school in 1965, Fred and a friend founded what is now Subway Sandwiches with just $1000. They wanted to provide an alternative to the typical fast-food hamburger. In 1988, *Venture* magazine recognized him as franchiser of the year. Subway was opening about 22 franchises a week.

Each of these businesses is an example of how an entrepreneur can take a fairly common aspect of human behavior and create a business. By simply putting a bit of a twist in a product or service that puts it more in tune with the market's needs than existing businesses, you may be on the road to having a viable new business venture. The examples also illustrate the point that perceptiveness may be more important than innovative capability. If you can identify a need, then you can probably find an innovative way to meet it. If you start with an innovative product, however, you may not be able to find people who want to buy it.

These examples illustrate the value of listening to the market. This approach is beneficial when trying to identify what types of goods and services have potential. Other approaches are also available.

The "Market-Area Saturation Approach" May Help Identify Opportunities. The market-area saturation approach involves looking at one or more cities to see if there is room for another business. Industry data shows that it usually takes a certain number of people to support each type of business. The following examples have been provided by the Census of Retail Trade on the average number of inhabitants per store:

Hardware stores—3000 people per store

Bookstores—26,000 people per store

Nursery and garden supply—26,000 people per store

Eating places—8500 people per store

Women's clothing—5000 people per store

Furniture stores—3000 people per store

Florists—8600 people per store

Barber shops—2200 people per store

If you want to see if an opportunity exists for a stationery store in a town with a population of 60,000 people, then check the data. Census data indicates there are 33,000 inhabitants per store. If the area already has three stationery stores, there may be little room or opportunity for another store.

A word of caution needs to be made here. Many businesses fail because they were started in a town where the owner lived or wanted to live. This restricts your opportunities and may be a fatal mistake for your business. As mentioned earlier, you cannot change the market. If you want to have the highest probability of success, you must be willing to locate your business where the customers are in search of a business—not where you want to live.

The market-area saturation approach is helpful as a quick indicator of a business opportunity, but it has numerous potential drawbacks. It does not take into consideration whether the existing stores are large or small, successful or unsuccessful, or whether they are independent, franchises, or part of a chain. The method also does not take into con-

sideration the exact locations, brands offered, or pricing strategy offered by the businesses. It also fails to take the nature of the population
into account. A town with a large number of retirees may be entirely
different from a town that is comprised primarily of blue-collar families, is oriented to tourists, or has a large university.

The "Segmentation Approach" May Help Identify "Gaps."   Another
way to identify business opportunities is called the "segmentation approach." With this technique you start by looking at the overall market
for a particular product or service. Next, you try to identify different
types (segments) of customers and the extent to which their needs are
being met. This approach may incorporate certain aspects of the
market-area saturation approach. Even if the market-area saturation
approach indicates there may already be enough businesses of that type,
specific opportunities may still exist if the area has a large number of
people with high levels of income who are not having their particular
needs met. This might be the case with Mary's Lawn and Garden Center. The segmentation approach may also reveal that a certain part of
the larger area has been growing rapidly and there is no business within
a five-minute drive to meet this segment's needs. This approach has
been popular for determining the need and location for neighborhood
convenience stores, pizza delivery services, car washes, etc.

This approach is particularly useful in identifying whether opportunities exist for specialty businesses such as French restaurants, gourmet
shops, travel agencies, yard services, etc. A particular group of people
(segment of the population) similar in terms of education, age, income,
market value of household, type of job, number of children living at
home, and other needs may have a propensity to be customers in search
of specific types of business.

The segmentation strategy is based on the notion that no business, no
matter how large, can be all things to all people at all times. Particular
groups of people have particular needs. Even if the number of businesses in a market appears to exceed the saturation point, sizeable opportunities may exist. The hotel-motel business illustrates this point.
Motel franchises have recently introduced "suites" for people who desire to meet with other people when they are traveling. One franchise
directs its advertising strategy primarily to female travelers. Even
though the number of hotels and motels appeared to be at the saturation level, the executives of the motel franchise found that this segment
of business travelers was still in search of a business that would offer
facilities more conducive to conducting business. This strategy was par-

ticularly attractive to women traveling alone. Their market research indicated that many women feel uncomfortable with traditional motel rooms. The traditional motel room with only a bed and bathroom did not meet some of the changing needs in the marketplace. A couple of other motel and hotel franchisers recognized that another segment of the market was not having its needs met. They found that people who may be staying more than a few days may also want a small kitchen so they do not have to go to restaurants for every meal.

These businesses recognized the existence of sizeable segments of people who want a motel to be an office while other people want it to be a home away from home. Instead of trying to be all things to all people, each franchise wanted to be the "best" to a specific segment of people. Business travelers with particular needs became the "target" market segment for each motel franchise.

Perceptiveness May Be More Important Than Inventiveness. The interesting point about all these examples is that none of the people or businesses which have been so successful "invented" their basic products or services. Ray Kroc did not invent the hamburger nor did Perry Mendel invent day care for kids. However, these entrepreneurs were perceptive and resourceful. They identified a problem in the market and turned it into a business opportunity.

Another way to develop a list of product or service ideas is to review issues for the last few years of popular entrepreneurial magazines such as *Inc.*, *Entrepreneur*, and *In Business*. These magazines provide numerous examples of new business ideas, emerging trends, and profiles of successful start-ups. The American Entrepreneurs Association (1-800-421-2300) may also be useful. It provides a catalog of manuals on how to start various businesses ranging from furniture stripping services, curb painting services, child care, videotaping, coupon mailing services, antique shops, do-it-yourself framing, used-book shops, and hundreds of other businesses.

Two other sources of information about new product ideas are worth noting. The *International New Product Newsletter* (612-426-6647) provides valuable information on license rights, distribution opportunities, and joint-venture possibilities for various new products. The U.S. Department of Commerce prints *Government Inventions for Licensing, An Abstract Newsletter*. This publication lists numerous inventions that offer licensing opportunities. This may be the "backwards" approach because it starts with a product rather than a market opportunity, but it will broaden your field of vision.

Step 3: Determining the Needed Capabilities and Resources

Now that you have listed problems in the marketplace and identified the corresponding business opportunities, the time has come to determine the needed capabilities and resources for each of the opportunities that seems to have merit. People often make the mistake of ruling out various opportunities as they develop and review the list generated in Step 2 because they are not familiar with that business or lack experience in it. They tend to investigate only the areas they already know as an employee or as a customer, or that they can learn in a short period of time.

At first glance, this appears to be a logical approach. By using this approach, however, an individual tends to overlook emerging opportunities or get involved in areas where the market could be saturated quickly. If you can get into a business that easily, then other people also can get into that type of business and become your competitors.

As noted in Step 2, you should be willing to investigate opportunities which may be new to you. You might say, "What about the need for experience in that type of business that was emphasized at the beginning of this book?" The interesting thing about the six-step process is that if you do a good job in Step 1, you may be able to spot emerging opportunities early—before other people even see them.

Prior experience is very important, but with sufficient lead time you may be able to gain the experience and education needed to have a chance to beat the odds. The H & R Block example illustrates the point. Henry and Richard Bloch were not certified public accountants nor did they need to be tax experts as they started Step 2. By identifying early the growing opportunity for individual tax preparation, they had enough time to study the market while learning about tax accounting and gain the necessary experience before starting H & R Block Tax Service.

This process can be accelerated in two ways. First, if you already have a strong background in starting and managing a business, you can hire specialists to deal with the "technical" side of the business. This is what the Blochs did. Second, you could bring in a partner with strong technical experience in that field instead of hiring someone. This is one of the principal reasons why many new businesses start as partnerships. A partner may be able to contribute valuable knowledge and experience as well as money to the business venture.

In Step 3, you review the list of potential opportunities generated in Step 2 by asking, "Which of these opportunities do I already have, or can I acquire (via learning, hiring, or partnership) the knowledge and experience necessary to create and maintain customers?" If you already have or can acquire what is needed before anyone else even recognizes the opportunity, you may be able to cultivate and capture a large portion of the market. It is interesting to note that few areas of business take years to learn. Most learning takes place in the first year. In one year you may learn 80 percent of what can be learned in five years of experience. The last 20 percent also is important. But if you are the first to enter the market, the first 80 percent may be enough to keep your head above water while you try to learn the other 20 percent.

If you sense an emerging opportunity early and commit yourself to learning as much as possible before you open your business, you will increase your ability to beat the odds. When competitors enter the market, they will not have the "experience" factor that will enable you to make better decisions. Remember, most new businesses fail because of trial-and-error management or the lack of a market opportunity. If you have the knowledge and experience and are prepared to offer the market segment you target what it wants, then you may be able to beat the odds.

Step 3 also addresses various other factors that may be prerequisites for starting a business. Most new ventures also have technological, equipment, legal, investment, and time requirements. Technological requirements are closely related to skill requirements. Technological requirements refers to how sophisticated the process may be for providing goods and services. Low- or no-technology businesses usually demand minimal skills and equipment. High-technology businesses usually require larger investments in equipment, take more lead time, and present difficulties in attracting qualified employees.

All of the elements in Step 3 tend to be interrelated. In certain cases, you may be able to substitute automated equipment for labor. In other cases, the technology may be covered by a patent and you will have to secure rights to use it. Under these conditions, it may take additional time as well as raise the amount of investment needed to start your business.

Step 3 is not intended to be a process where you must do an in-depth analysis of the prerequisite capabilities and resources. Instead, it is intended to have you take a look at whether there may be factors that will keep you from pursuing each opportunity. You may find after reviewing trade data that it usually takes $150,000 to start that type of business rather than the $60,000 you thought would be needed. You may find that one firm has exclusive patent rights and will not license the rights to its technology or equipment to anyone else. Conversely, you may also find that certain business opportunities that originally seemed complicated may be rather straightforward because equipment and skilled labor are readily available.

When you review the list of opportunities generated in Step 2, you may find that some of them may require considerable education or experience. If you do not have the time to learn the skills or find that no one with the capabilities you lack is available to hire or bring in as a partner, then you should drop that opportunity from the list. This is also the case if you find you cannot secure the essential resources.

Step 4: Projecting the Financial Dimensions of the Remaining Opportunities

The next step in identifying the right new business opportunity for you involves analyzing the financial side of the remaining opportunities. Step 4 involves determining the expected level of sales, expenses, profit, the initial capital requirement, and the projected cashflow for each business. Step 1 revealed that needs are not being met in the marketplace. Step 2 revealed there may be a way to transform the unmet needs into a business opportunity. Step 3 indicated that you have or can develop the capability to offer one or more segments of the market what it wants. Step 4 addresses whether you will be able to create and maintain customers for a sufficient level of profit to justify the effort, investment, and risk.

Step 4 attempts to answer three questions. The first question is, "How much money will it take to start each type of business?" The second question is, "What return (profit) on investment will each opportunity yield?" The third question is, "How soon will the business be able to generate a positive cashflow?" This question is critical because too many businesses run out of money before they can stand on their own. In Step 4, you are not only trying to identify the opportunities that will make a profit, you are trying to identify the ones that will justify the risk you (and possibly others) will be taking in time and money.

Step 4 is intended to eliminate the opportunities that do not have profit potential. Step 4 brings two particular points to the surface. First, it illustrates the need to have a good understanding of financial accounting. Second, it stresses the need to be concerned with starting a business that has the potential to make a reasonable profit and generate a positive cashflow soon after it opens its doors.

The second point often stirs controversy with some people who want to start their own business. They often say "being their own boss" or "interest in the products" is their primary concern. They say making a lot of money is important but it is a secondary concern. You may want to start a business for a lot of reasons, including meeting the challenge and being one's own boss, but go into this proposition with both eyes open. Your business will need to make a profit if you want to be your own boss and enjoy the lifestyle associated with having your own business.

In some cases, starting your own business is like courtship and marriage. There may be a lot of excitement at first, but in too many businesses and marriages, the honeymoon ends sooner than anyone had expected. The moral to the story is when you are thinking about starting a business, you may go into it for the fun of it, but before you begin be sure there will be a sufficient profit to keep you going if the fun ends. The emotions associated with doing something special are an integral part of human nature but they should not overshadow the need for your business to make a profit. The emotional side and your personal preferences will be addressed in Step 5 after you have projected each opportunity's relative financial merit.

Profit is not a dirty word. If your business is making money, you can handle the daily pressures more easily. Profit permits you to hire additional people to ease your own work load. Profit means that you may have money available to meet life's little surprises. Also, if you get to the point where you want to get out, a profitable business is easier to sell than one that has been shaky from the start. By all means, do not start a business as you would start a hobby; too much is at stake.

You should start a business that has the potential to make a good and lasting profit. Even the Internal Revenue Service makes this distinction. If you do not show a profit on a regular basis, the IRS may rule your business a "hobby" and not permit you to list your expenses as business deductions. You may have numerous reasons for starting a business. Profit does not need to be at the top of the list, but your venture's ability to yield a sufficient return needs to be on the list.

Two key considerations for Step 4, to justify the risk, are, "How much money are you and others willing to put into a business venture?" and "What is your desired return on investment?" The amount of money or capital required to start a business and what it will yield vary with each type of business. Fortunately, data on the amount of money required and the average return on investment data are usually available from trade associations and other financial sources.

The first step in learning more about the financial side of each type of business is to contact the corresponding trade association. Most large libraries have *The Encyclopedia of Associations* (Gale Research Company) and *National Trade and Professional Associations of the United States*, which list the addresses and phone numbers for various trade associations. Most trade associations calculate financial information from their members. In some cases, trade associations may provide you with this data free of charge. You can get additional information about certain types of businesses by looking through the *Business Periodicals In-*

dex and the *Magazine Index*, which are located in the reference section of most libraries. These indexes identify articles about various types of businesses that have appeared in the last few years. These articles may provide valuable information about market trends as well as current financial data. Six other sources of financial data are also worth reviewing. *Standard & Poor's Industry Surveys, National Cash Register's Expenses in Retail Business, Robert Morris Associates, Inc.'s Annual Statement Studies, Almanac of Business and Industrial Ratios, Business Profitability Ratios,* and *Financial Studies of the Small Business* provide key operating ratios for numerous types and sizes of businesses. The *U.S. Industrial Outlook*, published annually by the U.S. Department of Commerce, gives historical data, current estimates, and five-year projections for nearly 200 industries. Bankers and accountants also are in a position to provide additional financial information on various types of businesses.

After reviewing the various sources of financial information and doing some preliminary projections of possible levels of sales and expenses for each of the business opportunities that made it to Step 4, you should have a better idea of average profit levels, initial capital requirements, returns on investment, and the time it will take each type of business to pay its way. You should also have a rough estimate of whether you may need to borrow money, bring a partner in, or seek additional investors.

Step 4 is intended to provide an initial view of each business opportunity's relative financial merit. It would be an insurmountable task to do an in-depth financial analysis of a large number of business opportunities. This is why it is important for you to gather as much information from the corresponding trade associations and other sources of financial information. The more information you can get from external sources, the sooner you can move on to comparing the alternatives in Step 5.

Two points should be stressed at this time. First, one of the appeals of franchises is that most franchisers are in a position to provide financial information on their franchise units. This reduces the need to start from scratch when making financial projections. Second, you will need to do a more in-depth analysis of the business opportunity you select at the end of the six-step process as part of your business plan for that venture. Chapters 7 and 8 are designed to assist you with the more comprehensive financial projections.

At this time, you should be able to eliminate the opportunities that do not appear to have profit potential as well as those with an initial capital requirement beyond the amount you will be able to raise. It is hoped that some opportunities will be left for consideration in Step 5.

Step 5: Ranking the Opportunities in Terms of Personal Preferences, Financial Worthiness, and Perceived Risk

Each of the remaining business opportunities will now be ranked according to three important criteria: (1) personal preference, (2) financial worthiness, and (3) perceived risk. As noted earlier, your personal preferences are an important factor to consider when starting a business. However, your personal preferences have been postponed to this step for two reasons. First, your preferences would have limited the opportunities to what you know. Second, you may have been "seduced" by an opportunity that had limited, if any, profit potential. After all, few people enjoy having a business as they go into bankruptcy. You are more likely to enjoy having your own business if it is generating a healthy financial return.

You should rate each remaining opportunity on a scale of 1 to 5. Ask yourself, "Which of the business opportunities am I willing to invest my life in?" If you are excited about the prospect of spending 60 or more hours a week for the next 5 to 10 years without taking a vacation on a business opportunity, then give it 5 points. If you find the opportunity to be moderately interesting and would consider hiring someone else to run the business if you got bored, then give it 3 points. If after reviewing an opportunity you find it to be contrary to your interests and do not even want to be a limited partner in it, then drop it from your list.

Each opportunity should then be rated in terms of its financial worthiness. This involves establishing a "minimal profit or return on investment" objective. Even though the remaining opportunities at this point appear to have profit potential, you may need to eliminate the ventures that will not yield a sufficient level of profit to justify the risk. A good place to begin when trying to establish a "minimum return objective" is to determine the return you can get for your money if it was put in safe investments like five-year certificates of deposit or medium- to long-term government bonds.

If the current return or yield for these "safe" investments is 8 percent, then why should you risk your money for anything less than 8 percent? A good rule of thumb is that your minimum return on investment objective should be greater than the return associated with a "safe" investment. If you set your minimum return objective at 2 percentage points higher than the available safe type of investment return, then you would use a 10 percent return as the "threshold" for evaluating each business opportunity.

If your preliminary financial projections for the first five years for a business opportunity reveal the average annual return to be at least 30 percent, then give it 5 points. If the projected annual return is 2 to 3 percentage points over the threshold rate, then give it 3 points. Any business opportunity that appears to be unable to generate at least a 6 percent return on your investment before taxes should be dropped from the list. Even if you give it a 5 on the personal preference scale, you should think twice before considering the opportunity any further.

Remember, businesses make money; things that take your time and cost you money are "hobbies." Quite a few people consider lowering their minimum return objective because they really like that business opportunity. People are great rationalizers when they find business opportunities that look like they will be fun. Exercise some self-discipline from the beginning and make a contract with yourself not to start a business which will not achieve your minimal return objective.

The final criteria for Step 5 involves risk. Risk and financial return tend to be related. Generally speaking, the greater the risk, the greater the financial return if you succeed. Profit is defined as the reward for taking entrepreneurial risk. Step 5 takes risk into account by raising the questions, "Are there aspects to this business that are particularly risky?" You need to identify any areas that could jeopardize each opportunity. Particular attention needs to be directed to what are known as "fatal flaws." Nearly every business idea is based on a few assumptions. You assume a certain rate of technological change, certain economic conditions, certain legal factors, etc. The less things are susceptible to surprises or major disaster, the less risk.

If the business opportunity is almost certain to succeed and you consider your data to be sound, then give the opportunity 5 points. This would be the case if you had a patent to a product, had direct access to all the raw materials, and customers were already lined up with money in their hands to buy it. This is relatively rare; most business opportunities have their fair share of risk. Conversely, if the opportunity seems to have substantial risk associated with it at every turn, then you will have to give it a rating of 1 or 2.

Step 6: Selecting the Business Opportunity to Pursue

At this point you should be in a position to narrow down the list of opportunities to one or two potential ventures. Step 6 involves ranking each remaining opportunity on a 15-point scale. The 15-point scale gives each of the three factors (personal preference, financial worthiness, and perceived risk) equal weight. If you want to place more weight on personal preference, then you can either eliminate all opportunities that score less than 3 points on that dimension or double the points allocated to that dimension and rank the opportunities on a 20-point scale.

The ideal situation would be to have at least one opportunity score 5's on all three dimensions. This would be particularly appealing if the opportunity had a small initial capital requirement. Don't expect to find an opportunity this good; if it were that good, someone else would already be doing it or you overlooked something in your research.

Ranking the opportunities on the 15-point scale will direct your attention to the best opportunity for you at this time. It is hoped that the best opportunity scored at least 10 points on the 15-point scale with no dimension receiving a score of less than 3 points. If none of the opportunities scored 10 or more points, then you have three courses of action. You can accept the best opportunity, even though it scored less than 10 points. You should avoid this temptation. Don't be one of the people who say, "I've already made up my mind; don't confuse me with the facts." Too many people go into business because they didn't know better. Don't be one of the people who knew better but still went into business. Exercise self-discipline and avoid the temptation to rationalize away the situation by saying, "I'm sure that if I try hard, it will succeed. In this case, the old saying, "It is better to have loved and lost than to never have loved at all" does not apply. It is far better not to start a business that is destined to fail than to start one and fail.

Your second possible course of action would be to start the whole six-step process all over again. You may have missed some problems/opportunities in your initial analysis, or some new ones may have emerged since you started your analysis. The third possible course of action would be to view the time you invested in pursuing a business opportunity as a learning experience. To paraphrase a Kenny Rogers song, "Knowing when to hold them and when to fold them" is an important part of pursuing a business opportunity. It may turn out that there just isn't a good fit between present market needs and opportunities, your personal capabilities and preferences, your financial expectations, and your tolerance for risk. If this is the case, then it is natural to be frustrated with the time and money spent in your analysis. It may be advisable for you to invest your next couple of years learning more about business either through education or experience. You could then initiate the six-step process at a later date when conditions may be more favorable.

If the six-step process has identified an attractive opportunity, then you are now in a position to go on to the "seventh" step: developing the business plan. The following chapters describe the factors that need to be addressed as part of your "blueprint" for building a business that should give you a reasonable chance for beating the odds. As you will see, the time has come for you to roll up your sleeves, put some new batteries in your calculator, sharpen your pencil again, and do an in-depth analysis of the opportunity you have selected to pursue.

Entrepreneurial Qualities Self-Test: Part 2

1. What is the maximum amount of money I am willing to invest in the business?

    $ _____ .

2. What is the desired target return on my investment?

    _____ %

3. What is the minimum acceptable rate of return I will accept for my investment?

    _____ %

4. What are my strengths (education, training, experience, or personal qualities) for starting and managing a new business?

    a.

    b.

    c.

    d.

    e.

5. What are my weaknesses (education, training, experience, or personal qualities) for starting and managing a new business?

    a.

    b.

    c.

    d.

    e.

6. For each weakness, what do I plan to do to reduce it (education, experience, bring in a partner, hire an employee, etc.)?

    weakness   plan to reduce it

    a.

    b.

    c.

    d.

    e.

7. In terms of business skills, I rate my understanding of or experience in:

	None	Some	High
a. How the economy works, economic factors	1 2	3	4 5
b. Legal factors	1 2	3	4 5
c. Budgeting and profit planning	1 2	3	4 5
d. Financial management and control	1 2	3	4 5
e. Employee relations and personnel management			
	1 2	3	4 5
f. Managing day-to-day business operations	1 2	3	4 5
g. Buying and inventory control	1 2	3	4 5
h. Analyzing the marketplace	1 2	3	4 5
i. Determining which goods and services to offer	1 2	3	4 5
j. Promoting and advertising products or services			
	1 2	3	4 5
k. Location analysis	1 2	3	4 5
l. Pricing products or services	1 2	3	4 5

Total Points = _____

Scoring Breakdown for Question 7

1. If you have *more than 53 points*, then you have a very strong background. However, this will not guarantee you success. If you are entering a highly competitive marketplace, you will be competing against people who already know what does and does not work. A strong background is important, but it will still take time to learn all the ins and outs of the marketplace.

2. If you have *between 43 and 53 points*, then you may have a sufficient understanding about business to proceed to Chapter 3. If you have one or more areas that received a 1 or 2 rating, get additional training or experience. The marketplace does not reward trial-and-error learning on the job once you start your business.

3. If you have *less than 43 points* (an average of less than 3.5 points per area), then you have only a moderate understanding or an unbalanced understanding of the basic business concepts. You may not have sufficient depth or breadth of knowledge and experience to start and manage a new business. Consider additional training, work experience, bringing in a partner or manager with the needed skills, or buying a franchise that offers extensive training and assistance. In any event, you are not ready to start a business on your own at this time.

PART 2

Preparing Your Business Plan

3

The General Overview and Legal Structure

Now that you have identified the type of business opportunity you want to pursue it is time to begin preparing your business plan. Even though you have a general idea of the kind of business to start, numerous questions remain unanswered. The business plan provides a basis for the decisions that must still be made.

When people complete the six-step process described in Chapter 2, they often feel they do not need to prepare a formal business plan because they know what goods or services they want to offer to the one or more market segments they plan to serve. Getting to this point may have taken a lot of time, effort, and thought, but a lot still needs to be determined. Preparing a business plan helps to identify questions you need to answer. It also provides a framework and timetable for its implementation.

The probability of being successful in starting a new business is directly related to the extent your business plan is accurate and complete. Accordingly, it will take considerable time and effort to prepare a useful business plan. It may take at least four months to prepare a business plan for even the simplest new business. A note of caution also needs to be brought up at this time. Some people believe they do not need to prepare a business plan if they don't need to borrow money, bring in partners, or issue stock. This is a mistake. A business plan is not the same as a request for financing; it is your "blueprint" for building a successful business.

Anyone who tries to build anything, especially something as complicated as a business, without having a blueprint is courting disaster. It is true that a business plan may help you get financing for your business, but it is important for other reasons. A business plan is a reflection of your ability to manage. It identifies specifically the who, what, when, where, how much, why, and how of your proposed venture. If you do not have the patience, perseverance, skill, and information to prepare a business plan, then you probably lack the ability to start and manage a new business.

Most business plans have three basic components. They start with a general overview of the business, they discuss how the business will create and maintain customers, and they conclude with a set of financial projections that indicate the level of profit the business is expected to make in its first few years of operation. The following business plan outline identifies most of the items that should be addressed in a business start-up.

I. Executive Summary
II. Table of Contents
III. Overview of the Business Concept
    A. Identification of the market opportunity
    B. Growth and financial objectives for the business
    C. Discussion of the legal form of organization and ownership
    D. Profile of the management team and organization chart
    E. Description of the market(s) to be served and location for the business
    F. Basis for financing the business
    G. Timetable for establishing the business
IV. The Marketing Part of the Business Plan
    A. Description of the industry: an overview of its history, trends, and influential factors
    B. Analysis of immediate and potential competitors
    C. Profile of the target market(s) and geographic area to be served
    D. Presentation of the marketing mix for creating and maintaining customers
        1. Product-service strategy
        2. Price strategy
        3. Promotional strategy
        4. Physical distribution and location strategy
    E. Projected sales and market share
    F. Identification of any proprietary position, including patents, licenses, copyrights, franchise rights, exclusive agreements, etc.

V. The Financial Part of the Business Plan
   A. Projected initial capital requirement
   B. Projected opening day balance sheet
   C. Projected first year-end income statement
   D. Projected first year-end balance sheet
   E. Projected cashflow for the first year
   F. Projected income statements for the second through fifth years
   G. Projected balance sheets for the second through fifth years
   H. Key operating ratios
   I. Description of the sources of debt and equity financing for start-up and growth
   J. Projected return for the owners-investors
VI. Supplemental Factors
   A. Identification of risks and insurance coverage
   B. Identification of employee-related regulations and tax reporting requirements
   C. Identification of all legal factors, including licenses, taxes, zoning and building and reporting requirements.

The Executive Summary

A business plan begins with an executive summary. The executive summary is one or two pages in length and captures the essence of the proposed business venture. Even though it appears at the beginning of the plan, it is usually written after the rest of the plan has been completed.

The executive summary serves a very important purpose. It forces you to articulate the basic ingredients of your business venture. The executive summary can be viewed as what you would say if you had less than one minute to tell someone about your business. First-timers find this to be a challenge. Too often, they say, "I plan to start a family-oriented restaurant serving home-cooked food."

It is not unusual for bankers, potential partners or investors, suppliers, or friends to ask you about your proposed venture. The executive summary provides a very concise description of your business. The executive summary profiles the proposed business in terms of the specific market(s) to be served, the business's competitive advantage(s), its projected rate of growth, how it will be financed, and the projected return to its owner(s). It goes beyond generalities. The executive summary contains the vital facts about your business and reflects the research that went into preparing your business plan. If it is done well and it reflects a solid business proposal, anyone who reads it will want to read the entire business plan.

Overview of the Business Concept

This part of the business plan is devoted to identifying why the business is being started and what you expect it to become in five or more years. The overview of the business concept forces you to state what your objectives are, when you plan to achieve them, what risks you expect to encounter, and who will be involved in the venture.

Every successful business was formed to capitalize on a specific market opportunity. The first part of the business plan should identify the market opportunity. The opportunity could be something as simple as "to provide computer-controlled lawn sprinkler systems for a targeted market segment of upper-income homeowners in Landfall," a planned retirement community in Wilmington, North Carolina, to Fred Smith's concept, "to provide overnight delivery throughout the United States," which served as the basis for creating Federal Express. The description of the market opportunity will be fairly brief at this stage because it will be addressed in detail in the marketing part of the business plan.

The Objectives for the New Business

The next section of the business plan identifies the objectives for the business. As noted earlier, one of the benefits of starting your own business is that you can start it for any reason you desire. Your objectives could range from "making a 20 percent annual return after taxes on owner equity to be sustained over 10 years" to "providing jobs for all six members of my family until I retire."

In any event, it is important for you to state your objectives in specific terms. If you want to create a business that will have sales of $30 million and a net worth of $2 million, and be recognized as the leading firm in its field, then it needs to be stated in writing. If you plan to start a new type of venture, franchise it within 6 years, and have at least 100 franchisees in 10 years, then it needs to be stated. The same applies to having the objective of creating a business with patents that will be bought out by a Fortune 500 company for at least $5 million within 5 years. It does not make any difference if your objectives are to be on the cover of

Inc. magazine or just to have your business provide you with an after-tax income of $20,000 per year; your objectives need to be in writing and stated as specifically as possible.

Objectives can be viewed as "dreams with a deadline." They should be considered as desired destinations with a targeted date of arrival. You must avoid the temptation to say, "I want to make money" or "I want to have a growing business." These aren't objectives; they are merely directions. Objectives serve as the basis for all your business decisions. If your objectives are vague, then you will have difficulty deciding how much you will need to expand your operations as well as how to finance growth.

The Legal Form of Organization

You will need to decide early in the planning process which legal form of organization will be the most appropriate for your business. This turns out to be a multiple-choice question. Most businesses may operate in one of the following three legal forms of organization: the sole proprietorship, the partnership, or the corporation. Each prospective business owner should understand the characteristics associated with each form so that the most appropriate legal form of business is selected for that particular business.

The Sole-Proprietorship Form of Organization

The sole proprietorship is owned by one individual. Accordingly, the sole proprietor is his or her own boss and therefore usually makes or breaks the business. The legal implication associated with a proprietorship is that because the proprietor has sole control of the business, that person also has sole responsibility. Accordingly, legal and financial liabilities arising out of operating the business extend directly to the owner and are not limited to the business enterprise. This is the major disadvantage or risk associated with a noncorporate form of business. In a corporation, business liabilities usually stop with the business enterprise and do not extend to the owners of the business. Unlike corporations, proprietorships are easy to initiate, relatively free from government regulation, and may be subject to lower taxes.

In a proprietorship, all business income is treated and thereby taxed as personal income. Therefore, when the owner files an income tax return, a schedule showing the revenues and expenses of the business operation is included. The net income or loss is added or subtracted from any other income the sole proprietor reports on the tax return. The relative simplicity of forming and operating this form of business may explain why nearly 75 percent of all businesses in the United States are sole proprietorships.

If you choose to start your business as a sole proprietorship, then remember to do three things. First, you should check to see if you need to register your business in the state and county where you plan to locate your business. In most cases, you will also need to file a "DBA," or "doing business as," form. In some states, this is called a "certificate of assumed name." This form indicates who is the proprietor of the business, if someone wants to initiate legal action against the business. You will be expected to file this form unless the name of your business is identical to that which appears on your official personal records. If your name is Susan Reeves Smith and you plan to call your business "Susan Smith's Auto Repair," then you will still have to file a DBA form. The same is true if the business will be called "The All American Auto Repair Shoppe." You should also check with your state's Department of Commerce, county office, or city hall to see if you will need to secure a "privilege license."

Second, attorneys usually recommend that you prepare a "right of survivorship" document. In some states, if you die, your business must be liquidated because technically you were the business. Therefore, the business can no longer exist. The right of survivorship gives you a vehicle for indicating what should be done with the business. Certain states will permit you to include the disposition of the business's assets in your will. The beneficiaries are then free to continue the business, sell it, or liquidate the assets as they see fit. This may keep probate proceedings from freezing the assets you have tied up in the business.

Third, you may consider designating someone, possibly an employee or your spouse, as your "agent." If you expect to be away from the business for extended periods of time, it may be worthwhile to give someone you trust the legal right to act in your behalf. This is similar to granting someone "power of attorney" to act in your behalf. Job descriptions for your employees are another way of authorizing certain people to do certain things. In some states, if your spouse is involved in the business, then the business may be considered to be a partnership rather than a sole proprietorship.

The agency relationship may be particularly worthwhile if you were to become mentally impaired. The agency agreement may be drafted in a manner that permits someone to conduct any or all aspects of the business until you get better or until the business can be concluded in a constructive manner. The right of survivorship and agency relationship are very important. If you plan to do them, don't put them off until later. Life is full of surprises and it would be a shame for your business to be liquidated if something bad happened to you. If you are going to put a significant part of your life into your business, then take a few legal precautions to be sure it can withstand your misfortune.

Finally, you should check with your state's Department of Commerce, county clerk, and city hall to find out what permits, licenses, and taxes you will need to have to start your business. Your accountant will also be in a position to identify various tax requirements such as applying for your employer identification number, withholding employee wages for income taxes, social security, and unemployment compensation changes, as well as your own self-employment obligations to the federal government. Your accountant will also indicate various recordkeeping requirements and procedures. Your attorney should also be consulted. He or she will identify various licensing requirements and recommend certain ideas for starting your business that are related to estate planning.

The Partnership Form of Organization

The partnership is a noncorporate form of business having two or more owners. Partnerships exist when at least two people "formally" combine their ideas, talents, or capital for business purposes. A partnership is in many ways similar to a proprietorship. Legal and financial liabilities extend beyond the business enterprise to include the owners. If the business defaults on any of its obligations, then creditors generally can look to any of the partners individually to satisfy the obligations of the business. Accordingly, if a creditor of a partnership seeks to collect what is due from a partner and is unsuccessful, then the creditor may seek to collect the entire amount from any one of the partners without regard to what share of the business that particular partner owns. It would then be up to that partner to seek restitution from the other partner(s). From a tax point of view, partnerships are taxed like proprietorships. Partners are taxed on their share of the partnership's profit at their income tax rate as personal income. Partners are expected to pay their own self-employment social security tax.

Because of the division of profits and the liabilities associated with a partnership, it is strongly recommended that prospective partners use the services of an attorney to draw up a written partnership agreement. Such a contract should spell out each partner's respective rights and duties. One other legal factor needs to be noted. The death, withdrawal, or addition of a partner automatically and legally terminates the original partnership agreement. Accordingly, expansion, dissolution, and buy-out arrangements should be agreed to in advance to minimize problems that may arise at a later date.

A partnership will also be expected to be registered in the county where the business will be located. It may also be required to file a DBA or assumed-name form. Partnerships may also be required to secure a "privilege license" by the state or county. The right of survivorship and agency relationship documents usually are of little value because of the nature of a partnership. The reluctance of people to be held liable for the actions of the other partners and the difficulty in adding or deleting partners may explain why less than 10 percent of the businesses in the United States are partnerships.

The partnership just described is considered a "general" partnership. Each partner has unlimited liability. A partnership may be formed where one or more of the partners can be a "limited" partner. A person can be a limited partner if the partnership agreement indicates that person's involvement in the business to be purely financial. Under no circumstances can a limited partner be involved in any of the business's decisions. The limited partner's liability is thus limited to the amount of money that person invests in the business.

If a limited partner becomes involved in the business decision processes, then the courts may declare that person to be a general partner with unlimited liability. The limited partner may have limited liability, but she or he also has a limited opportunity to express thoughts about how to improve the business. This can be particularly frustrating if the business gets into financial trouble.

The major advantage of the limited-partnership arrangement is that it may provide a means for other people to invest in the business without having to form a corporation. As someone once said, "The best partner is a silent partner!" If all your partners are limited partners, then you get the benefit of their money without having to consult them as you would general partners when decisions need to be made. For this to happen, however, they would have to believe in your business concept and trust your business judgment.

The limited partnership has merit from a legal and financial perspective. Unlike the general partnership, if a limited partner dies, that person's share of the partnership is usually acquired by the remaining partners by some prearranged formula. It also may be possible for limited partners to transfer their ownership interests without dissolving the partnership. The limited form of partnership nevertheless does not relieve every partner of unlimited personal liability. At least one of the partners must be a "general" partner. If you are going to be making business decisions, then you will be a general partner. You will have the same unlimited liability as if the business were a general partnership or a sole proprietorship.

The Corporate Form of Organization

Corporations differ from proprietorships and partnerships in many ways. First of all, a corporation is considered a "legal entity." The corporation is treated as something separate from its owners. If a corporation is sued, defaults on its loans, or goes bankrupt, then the shareholders' losses cannot exceed the amount of money they invested in the firm. This means that the stockholders have limited liability. As stated earlier, sole proprietors and general partners have unlimited liability.

If you choose the corporate form for your business venture, you may find that you may still be personally liable for its affairs. Banks and other creditors may expect you to personally cosign any loans or other business agreements. Most new corporations do not have much money to meet their financial obligations. For this reason, the power company, phone company, and some of your suppliers may ask the major stockholders to be personally liable for fulfilling credit obligations if the corporation becomes insolvent.

The stockholders can be personally liable for the actions of the corporation for at least two other reasons. First, if the firm fails to conduct its affairs as a corporation, then it may be treated as if it were a proprietorship or partnership. The stockholders, through the firm's board of directors, must adopt bylaws, conduct regular meetings, elect officers, and keep records of the meetings. If they fail to do so, then the Internal Revenue Service or other creditors may request that the courts declare the owners of the business to be held personally liable for claims. The other instance of unlimited personal liability for the stockholders exists when they are involved in any criminal activity when conducting the corporation's affairs. This type of situation is rare, but it is quite clear that the owners' personal liability is limited only when they behave in the appropriate and legal manner.

Corporations have appeal because they limit the stockholders' legal and financial liabilities. Yet the corporate form has three major drawbacks. First, it takes more money to start a business as a corporation. The incorporation process tends to cost hundreds to thousands of dollars. Second, it takes more time and paperwork. You must file your "Articles of Incorporation" with the secretary of state where you plan to conduct your business, register the firm where its principal office is to be located or its real estate is to be held, elect directors, establish bylaws, issue stock, conduct meetings, and keep formal records of corporate decisions.

The major drawback to the corporate form is in the area of taxes. Profits are subject to "double taxation" because corporations are legal entities. The corporation will pay a federal tax on each year's profits to the Internal Revenue Service. Most firms are also required to pay a state income tax on their profits. The corporate income tax is the first "wave" of tax imposed on a firm's profits. The second wave occurs if the corporation's board of directors decides to distribute any of that year's profits left after state and federal taxes are paid. Stockholders are obligated to pay federal and state personal income taxes on dividends they receive from the firm. Corporate profits are taxed twice: once at the corporate level and then again as dividends at the stockholder level. As you can see, the benefits of limited personal liability come at the cost of double taxation.

A major advantage of the corporate form over partnerships and sole proprietorships goes back to the fact that a corporation is a legal entity. Whenever a partner or sole proprietor dies, the business also ceases. In a similar fashion, whenever a new partner is added or a partner wants to leave, a new partnership must be formed. This is not the case with the corporate form. If someone wants to become an owner of a corporation, then that person buys stock. Sale of stock transfers ownership from seller to buyer. Stockholders can come and go without affecting the legal status or operations of the firm. Moreover, if the corporation needs money to expand its operations or pay off debt, funds can usually be raised by selling additional stock.

The "Subchapter S," or "Sub S," corporation represents a special type of corporation that may appeal to people who plan to start a small business. The Sub S corporation is frequently referred to as "the corporation that is taxed like a partnership or proprietorship." This is not exactly the case, but there are some similarities. Your accountant should be in a good position to identify the merits of forming your business as a Sub S corporation.

The Sub S type of corporation does not pay a federal corporate income tax. Instead, the stockholders report their share (percent of ownership in the firm) of the corporation's profit for that year. For example, if you own one-half of the shares of stock in a Sub S firm that made $20,000 that year, then you would report Sub S income of $10,000 on your personal federal tax return. In a regular corporation, the firm pays a federal tax on its profits and the stockholders pay tax only on the dividends they receive. In the Sub S corporation, the firm does not pay a federal tax, but the stockholders pay a tax on the firm's profit rather than on the dividends they receive. In a sense, Sub S stockholders pay the corporate federal tax at their personal rate on their federal tax returns.

Many states charge a corporate income tax. The Sub S distinction is made at the federal tax level. Some states treat Sub S corporations as regular corporations. These states thereby tax the stockholders only for the dividends they receive.

The Sub S status has certain benefits but it also has certain restrictions. The IRS limits the number of people who can own stock in the business. The "S" indicates that only a "small" number of people can own stock in the corporation. The 1986 Tax Reform Act set a limit of 35 stockholders for a Sub S corporation. Moreover, the Sub S corporation can only issue one type of stock. In a general corporation you can have common stock and preferred stock, voting and nonvoting stock, and cumulative and noncumulative stock. The Sub S firm does not have this latitude.

There are many things to consider when you select the legal form for your business. Fortunately, you may be able to change the legal form after you start your business, if you meet certain requirements. Nevertheless, you should give this decision the time and attention it deserves. The legal form for your business will affect your initial capital requirement, your ability to raise money, your personal liability, how profits will be reported, the tax obligation you will incur, the cashflow for your business, and how you conduct your business.

You may find it helpful to ask yourself, "Which legal form will be the most appropriate in three to five years?" This will give you a good idea which legal form should be selected to start your business. Businesses that are expected to grow and need additional funds are usually formed as corporations. Most medium-sized businesses and nearly all large businesses are corporations. According to the *Statistical Abstract of the United States*, about 15 percent of businesses are corporations. However, corporations represent nearly 90 percent of sales. Even though 75 percent of the businesses are proprietorships, they account for only 7 percent of sales. Partnerships account for only 3 percent of sales. In any event, it is advisable for you to seek the advice of a certified public accountant, an attorney, a banker, and oftentimes, a business consultant before deciding how to structure your business.

Profile of the Management Team and Organization Chart

This part of the business plan will indicate whether the business venture has a good chance for beating the odds. The business plan needs to demonstrate that a marketing opportunity exists and that the people who will be involved in the business will be able to capitalize on that opportunity.

One of the facts of business life is that a business cannot be better than the people in it. If the primary reason for business failure is mismanagement, then you will need to show that you have stacked the deck in your favor. This section of the business plan should identify who will be involved in the business, what role they will play in its operations, and what position they will be in to increase the business's chances for success.

Take a close look at who you plan to have as part of your business. If their previous experiences will reduce trial-and-error processes and they will be bringing skills that will supplement your own strengths and minimize your weaknesses, then you should be in good shape. If you plan to hire friends and relatives just because they are friends and relatives, then you should step back and ask yourself if you are trying to start a viable business or a social club.

Businesses succeed because they are run by people whose decisions are better than their competitors' decisions. Be sure that you put together a team that will give you a competitive advantage. When you bring capable and experienced people into your business, your business will be able to "hit the ground running!" One of the advantages of buying a successful business is that its people have already demonstrated their ability to make the right decisions. Part of the price you pay when you buy an existing business is for "goodwill." Good people represent a significant part of the goodwill. If you start your business with experienced people, then you will be starting with goodwill. This increases your chances for beating the odds.

This section of the business plan should include an organization chart that shows which positions need to be filled, who will be in each position, and how many people will be employed in the first year of operation (see Figure 3-1). The salary and fringe benefits for each position should also be indicated. Job descriptions should reflect how the work will be divided. The organization chart should indicate how the jobs will be coordinated.

The business plan should also include a brief profile of the people who will play an influential role in the business. Each person's biographic sketch should indicate why this person was selected and any relevant background. Particular attention should be directed to past experience and education. Each person's résumé should be included in the appendix of the business plan.

The need for a management "team" has gained attention in recent years. There are so many different dimensions to starting and manag-

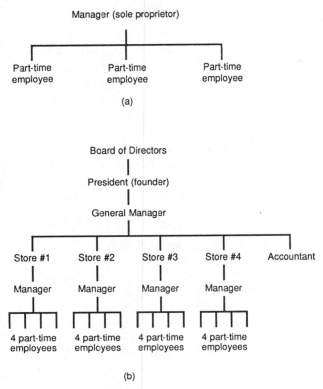

Figure 3-1. (a) Example of the first year's organization chart;
(b) example of the fifth year's organization chart.

ing a business that no one person can learn or do all of them well. When one person tries to wear all the "hats" and be the "Jack of all trades," things quickly fall through the cracks. Most "one-man shows" either remain one-person businesses or cease being businesses altogether.

If you want your business to grow and prosper, then you will need to have a team of people who know what needs to be done and who will do their jobs well. Pricing decisions will need to be made by people who understand the market and your business's costs. Budgets will need to be prepared by people who understand cost-volume-profit relationships. As the business grows, your job will be to coordinate the people who make the technical decisions.

If you are the sole proprietor, then you will need to indicate if other people will be employed and what their responsibilities will be. If you plan to start your business as a partnership, then you will need to indicate the division of work between the partners. Your partnership agreement should state specifically which partner will be responsible for selling, ordering inventory, hiring personnel, writing checks, etc. A survey by the Smaller Business Association of New England revealed that among their members, two-thirds of the partnerships had broken up. The primary reason for the breakups was changing interests or interpersonal conflict among the team members. It is important that each person's duties and responsibilities be determined in advance. This part of the business plan helps clarify the division of work and the division of management as well as identify potential areas of overlap, duplication, or weakness. Each partner's right to increase, decrease, or even sell his or her part of the business needs to be stated in this part of the business plan.

If you will be using the corporate form of organization, then the business plan should also profile who will be serving on the firm's board of directors. Most states require that the board be comprised of at least three people. Since the board is elected by the stockholders, it is not uncommon to find the major stockholders on the board. Nevertheless, the board should provide additional strength to your management team. It is advisable to have people on the board who will provide a sense of direction, who will be candid in their review of operations, and who will contribute valuable advice to the management team. Your board should have at least one person on it who has started a business from scratch and guided its growth for at least five years. This person may keep you from committing many of the classic mistakes made by first-timers.

If you do not go the corporate route, you should consider setting up an "advisory board" to help you make better decisions. Your advisory board can be made up of businesspeople who you respect in your community. You will probably have to pay them for their time, but you may find that they welcome the opportunity. In any event, the résumés for the people who will serve on your board should be included in the appendix. This part of the business plan may also identify who will serve as legal counsel and who will be the accountant for the business.

If you plan to grow, then your plan should reflect how the business will grow in terms of the number and nature of positions and jobs as well. It may be worthwhile to include a "projected organization chart" in your plan that reflects the way you expect the business to look in five years. Your objectives should be set in a five-year time frame, and your financial projections will be for the first five years. You should be able to show the organization what will be needed to achieve those goals and what served as a basis for the employment expenses included in your projected income statements.

Description of the Market(s) to Be Served and Location for the Business

This part of the general overview describes the basic thrust of your marketing efforts. The general overview identifies: (1) the goods or services you will be offering, (2) the type of customers you will be trying to attract, (3) the geographic territory you will be trying to serve, (4) whether you will be operating out of more than one facility, (5) if your business will be a franchise, (6) if you will have the exclusive rights to a particular brand, and (7) what you plan to have as your competitive advantage.

This section can be viewed as a "preview" to the marketing plan. The marketing plan will discuss each area in more detail. You may describe your marketing efforts in the following manner.

Early Childhood Development Center (ECDC) is designed to meet the needs of parents who want their pre-kindergarten-age children to experience various aspects of learning not available in "traditional" preschools. Many people of the "baby boom" generation have become parents. A significant number of these parents want their children to be enrolled in an ongoing program that will enhance their children's personal development. Industry data reveals that a substantial opportunity exists for a "developmental learning center." Traditional preschools are expected to grow 3 to 4 percent per year, whereas developmental centers are expected to grow between 10 to 20 percent per year for the next decade.

Most preschools are day-care centers. They have grown in popularity because they have offered working mothers an alternative to hiring a baby-sitter while they are at work. ECDC is not intended to compete with the traditional day-care business. Instead, it is designed to provide experiences that will permit children to grow as individuals and to be "ahead in the game" when they start regular school.

ECDC's developmental experiences will include computers, foreign languages, and performing arts. Field trips will also be offered on a regular basis. ECDC's staff will be selected for their background and education. Each staff member will have a degree in early childhood development.

Enrollment in ECDC will be limited to 110 children. The limited enrollment will assure parents that their children will receive individual attention. There will be two classes for each one-year-, two-year-, three-year-, and four-year-old group. Each of the two 1-year-old classes will be limited to 10 children. The other age groups will have a limit of 15 children per class.

Tuition for each child will be $550 per month for the nine-month academic year. A summer session will also be available at the same monthly rate. This rate is twice the typical preschool rate, but ECDC is not the typical preschool nor is it directed to the typical parents. ECDC is targeted to children whose parents have an income in excess of $70,000 per year and who want their children to attend a "developmental program" even if the wife does not have a full-time job.

The Norfolk, Virginia, metropolitan area has been selected for ECDC's first facility. A market study indicated that a growing number of young professionals are moving to the Norfolk metropolitan area because of its diversified economic base and proximity to the Atlantic Ocean. The market study also revealed that few preschools exist that offer the "developmental" approach.

ECDC plans to build a 6000-square-foot-facility on a 2½-acre site in a suburban location. Two acres will be used for the development center. The other half acre will become ECDC's headquarters as it expands its operations. The site was selected because it is within a five-minute drive for two of the most popular residential neighborhoods for young professionals in the Norfolk area.

ECDC plans to expand its operations to other cities with populations of at least a quarter-million people in the Mid-Atlantic area. The five-year plan calls for building two additional facilities in the Tidewater area of Norfolk, Hampton Roads, and Newport News in the second year. ECDC is expected to have 15 facilities by the end of the fifth year. Expansion plans include at least two facilities each in Charlotte, Greensboro, and Raleigh, North Carolina; in Baltimore, Maryland; and in suburban Washington, D.C.

ECDC's marketing goal is to operate at 85 percent capacity or 94 children per facility during the academic year and 50 percent capacity during the summer session. ECDC is expected to generate $8,340,750 annual sales in uninflated dollars ($6,979,500 for the academic year and $1,361,250 for the summer session) for its fifth year of operations when it has 15 facilities in operation.

If ECDC's management believes the market will continue to be strong for at least another decade, then ECDC will continue adding on the average of four new facilities per year. ECDC's long-range plans may include expanding their facilities to include kindergarten through the eighth grade. ECDC's overall marketing plan is to maintain ownership and management of its facilities rather than to franchise its operations. This strategy may slow ECDC's growth, but it should enable management to maintain the quality of its development programs and facilities. This will be essential if ECDC is to fulfill its 10-year goal of being recognized as the leader in offering experientially based, individualized development programs for preschool-aged children."

Basis for Financing
the Business

The general overview should identify how much money will be needed to start the business and how it will be financed. Chapter 7 provides a basis for estimating your business's initial capital requirement. Chapter 8 indicates the basic configuration of your business's assets, liabilities, and owner equity. The general overview summarizes the financial projections for Chapters 7 and 8.

If you plan to start your business as a sole proprietorship and finance it with your own money, then this section of the general overview will be a statement such as

> Johnson's Auto Repair will have an initial capital requirement of $26,500. It will be funded by Suzie Johnson, the sole proprietor, with money currently held in a six-month certificate of deposit.

If your business will be formed as a partnership, then the overview should reflect the partnership agreement, which states who is putting in how much money, who, if anyone, will be a limited partner, and how much money, if any, will be borrowed to start the business. The following statement reflects such an agreement:

> S.J.T. Specialty Products will have an initial capital requirement of $46,000. It will be funded in the following manner:
>
> $10,000 by John Smith—a general partner
> $10,000 by Paula Jones—a general partner
> $10,000 by Allison Taylor—a limited partner
> $16,000 by a five-year secured note from the American National Bank with monthly principal and interest payments with a 13 percent APR

If the business will be started as a corporation, then the overview should indicate how much of the firm will be financed via stock and debt. The basis for funding may be reflected in the following manner:

> Amalgamated Enterprises, Inc., will have an initial capital requirement of $120,000. Initial funding will be provided by the issue of 80,000 shares of common stock at $1 per share. The following people will serve as the initial stockholders:
>
> 25,000 shares—Irving Stevens
> 25,000 shares—Helen Brown
> 15,000 shares—Steve Johnson
> 15,000 shares—Bill Cohen

A $40,000 five-year secured note from American National Bank with a 13.75 percent APR will also be used to finance the business. The note calls for interest payments due on a monthly basis and a balloon payment for the principal of the note due at the end of the five-year term.

As you can see, the basis for financing the business depends on the legal side of the business, the amount of money to be raised, and whether the business will be funded by its owners-investors or by a loan. The basis for funding could also include short-term trade credit from one or more of the suppliers of inventory or equipment. This type of financing should also be noted in the general overview.

The general overview should also indicate if the business will need additional funding at a later date. If the business plans to expand its operations, retire a short-term note, or buy back stock from its stock-holders, then the overview should indicate when this is likely to occur, the amount of money involved, and how it will be funded.

Timetable for Establishing the Business

A considerable amount of time goes into starting a business. You will need to identify all the activities that will have to be completed and how long each will take, and determine the sequential nature of them.

The general overview should include the date you plan to open your business and the schedule of activities that are prerequisite to that target date. The timetable usually starts with a period for identifying market problems. It will be followed by a period for the analysis of each problem to determine if it represents an opportunity. Another block of time will need to be allocated to select the opportunity that will serve as the "core" of your new business venture. These three steps could take from three months to a couple of years.

Your timetable will need to reflect numerous other activities. Some of them will only take a couple of days. Other activities may take weeks or months. Your timetable will include: (1) finding the right target market and geographic area to serve, (2) determining the optimal type and size of your facility, (3) identifying potential locations, (4) selecting the appropriate site, and (5) negotiating the terms of the lease or building the facility.

If you will be making your own product, then you need to contact machinery vendors and allow sufficient time for delivery and installation. The same applies if you will be a retail business. You will need to determine which brands to carry, contact the suppliers to see if they will do business with you, place your orders, and allow enough time for the orders to be delivered before you open your doors to the public.

You will also need to advertise for any employees, interview people, check their backgrounds, and train them before they come into contact with your customers. The timetable also needs to reflect the time it takes to have your sign, letterhead, business cards, etc., made and shipped. Your grand opening advertising will also be planned and scheduled. If your promotion plan includes any "teaser" advertising that lets potential customers know about your business months before it opens, then your timetable will have to include this too. Teaser advertising can make a big difference in your first few months' sales and cashflow.

Starting a business may take more time and work than managing a business. You will need to identify what will need to be done, how long it will take, how much money you will need, and when you will need to pay for each facet of the business.

Anyone who is thinking about starting a business should keep Murphy's Law in mind at all times. According to Murphy, "If anything can go wrong, it will." Suppliers will not ship items on time. If they do, they may send the wrong type or number. Employees may quit after you have trained them but before you open for business. Construction of the "perfect" new building you leased may be delayed three weeks, thereby allowing you only one week to move in before opening day.

Your business should be based on good ideas. Yet ideas alone will not assure success. Timing is important, too. You need to be sure that you open your business at the right time of year. You also need more than a "To Do" list to orchestrate the various activities. A timetable will increase the probability that the right things happen at the right time.

Many new businesses start off on the wrong foot because their managers forget to do something or they miss a deadline. For example, many first-timers miss having their businesses listed in the phone book and yellow pages. The phone book may be distributed each summer, but the deadline for finalizing your contract and providing your yellow pages layout may be in January or February. You may not plan to open your business until August, but you will need to have the answers to numerous questions in January if you want to have your business featured in the yellow pages when your business opens its doors. By January, you will need to have: (1) selected the name for your business, (2) reached an agreement on your lease, (3) gained approval from your vendors to supply the brands you want to offer, (4) received authorization to handle various credit cards, and (5) decided on the hours you will be open.

The actual process of finalizing your phone and yellow page listings may take only a small amount of time, but if you don't have the right information before the deadline, you may miss out on what may be an essential part of your marketing plan. Quite a few of your prospective customers "let their fingers do the walking." It is difficult enough for a new business to attract customers; if you miss the phone listing deadline, you will be stacking the deck against your business before you even open its doors. Business visibility and viability go hand in hand.

The phone listing will not guarantee success, but not having it when you open your doors will most certainly result in failure. The same situation may apply to various other activities that will need to be identified, planned, and scheduled.

Mismanagement is the primary reason for new-business failure. If you plan ahead, then you may be able to identify potential problems and prevent them before they can jeopardize your business. Life is full of surprises and few things will go as planned. Nevertheless, if you have a plan with a timetable and are a flexible and resourceful individual, then you may still be able to get a few nights' sleep before you open your business.

The General Overview Helps You Think Things Through

It should be apparent from the preceding discussion of the general overview that preparing a business plan is not something that can be done overnight. The plan forces you to put your business concept into specific terms. To paraphrase George Odiorne, a noted management professor, consultant, and author, "If you can't put your ideas into words, dates, and dollars, then you don't know what you are talking about and should forget it rather than wasting any more of your time." The general overview is valuable because it helps you clarify what you have in mind. It is also helpful because it gives other interested parties a good idea of what will be involved in your proposed business venture.

4
Selecting the Right Target Market

The marketing part of your business plan describes how you will attempt to create and maintain customers for a profit. At this time, you need to describe your industry, your market, your competition, your prospective customers, and your marketing mix. This is important because no business operates in a vacuum. Your business plan must reflect the unique environment you will be operating in as well as what you plan to be your competitive advantage.

Our free-enterprise system encourages competition. This usually means it is a buyer's market rather than a seller's. If you do not offer what the market desires and are no better than your competition, then you are destined to fail.

To succeed, your business must offer what your competitors don't offer at all or well enough for the desires of the market. You must provide prospective customers a very good reason to go out of their way, to bypass your competition, and to give you their money. If your business activities are simply going to be a lukewarm rehash of what the person down the street is doing, then you had better reserve some space in the obituary section of the newspaper for your business.

Today's new business cannot be run-of-the-mill. There is simply too much competition for the consumers' dollars—and the consumers know it. If you are not in position to offer exactly what consumers want, as well as when, how, and where they want it, at a price they feel is fair, and still make a profit, then you should forget the whole thing.

The marketing part of the business plan begins with the identification of consumer wants that are not being met at all or well enough. The process of "listening" to the market in general terms was discussed earlier. Now you need to get down to the specifics.

First, you need to research the market and territory you selected in Step 6 in the process of identifying new business opportunities discussed in Chapter 2. You will need to study the nature of your industry, analyze your market, and develop your marketing mix.

Studying the Industry

Before you start any kind of business you need to have an in-depth understanding of the industry you will be in. You should join the trade association for your type of business. Check the *Encyclopedia of Associations* and *National Trade and Professional Associations in the United States* for a listing of trade associations for your type of business. A trade association is made up of people who are in that type of business as well as people who are suppliers to businesses in that trade. The trade association and its members have a wealth of information that they have gained via extensive experience in that type of business. What they know and what you can learn from them will definitely increase your odds for being successful. Most trade associations offer magazines or newsletters. They also schedule exhibits and speakers on a variety of topics to assist their members.

You should also gather information about trends for your industry's products, services, expenses, advertising, credit policies, rate of growth, foreign factors, current laws, pending regulations, technological changes, etc. *Standard & Poor's Industry Survey* profiles 45 major industries. *U.S. Industrial Outlook*, published by the U.S. Department of Commerce, has a section on emerging industries. *The Business Periodicals Index* and *The Magazine Index* may also identify articles about trends in your type of business. *The Small Business Sourcebook, The Encyclopedia of Business Information Sources*, and *Findex: A Directory of Market Research Reports, Studies, and Surveys* may also be helpful.

It is important for you to know whether you are about to enter an industry experiencing growth and increasing profitability versus one that is mature and saturated, if the industry is inflation- or interest-rate sensitive, whether chains and franchises dominate the market, if the industry is susceptible to foreign competition, if it is subject to major technological change, who are the major suppliers and customers, as well as what the future may hold. By understanding the nature of your industry you will be in a better position to analyze the specific market you are planning to enter. You will also be in a better position to identify ways to develop your competitive advantage.

Analyzing Your Market

At this time you need to study the specific geographic area where you plan to start your business. You want to learn about the unique nature of your area. You need to know about the population, the overall level and rate of growth of business activity, whether people move frequently and to what neighborhoods, if the downtown area is the center of business activity, if new suburban malls are planned, what are the major employers and whether they have a promising future, and various other factors that may affect business conditions in general and the type of business you plan to start in particular. Census data and the local chamber of commerce can be helpful here. You will be looking for the level of disposable income and whether the population has exhibited a willingness to try new products, services, and businesses.

One of the most important parts of your market analysis involves identifying the people or businesses who may have a desire to purchase your type of product or service. Your overall geographic market may comprise hundreds or even thousands of people who may have an interest in your product or service. You are trying to identify the number of potential customers, who they are, how often they buy, who they are currently buying from, how much they spend, and if they are brand or store loyal.

You want to learn which people are satisfied customers and which ones are still in search of a business. It will also be beneficial to learn how much money is spent on the type of goods and services you will offer in your geographic area. The *Census of Business,* which is conducted every five years in the years ending in 2 or 7, provides information for various businesses.

By gathering this data, you will be able to learn who buys what, how often, from whom, and what they may be looking for. No single business can be all things to all the people. Even though each customer may be unique, a number of people in most markets have some common interests. Just as a jigsaw puzzle is made up of different pieces, most markets are made up of different "segments" or groups of people (see Figure 4-1). Each segment is made up of people who have common features or interests. By analyzing the market, you will be in a position to identify the people who consume your type of goods and services,

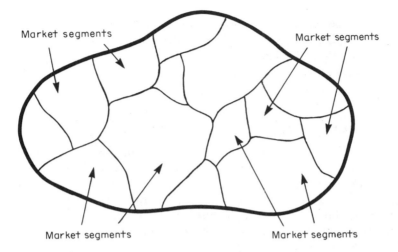

Figure 4-1. Market segmentation. Each market consists of numerous segments.

classify the market into various segments, ascertain which segments are still in search of a business, and determine which segments should be the target market(s) for your business.

Competitive Analysis

The next step in analyzing your market involves a complete analysis of the businesses already offering your type of goods and services in the geographic area under consideration. You want to learn how many businesses are already in the marketplace, what they offer, and where they are located. Once you have gathered this data, you will be able to develop a competitive "matrix" (see Figures 4-2 and 4-3) that reflects the strengths and weaknesses of the businesses in the market.

The competitive matrix is constructed by listing all the businesses vying for customers in a particular geographic area, identifying all the dimensions of their market offerings known as the marketing mix, and then rating each business on a scale of 1 to 5 in terms of its relative strength in each dimension. The competitive matrix provides a picture of where competition is strong as well as the areas where few, if any, businesses may be meeting the market's needs.

The next step involves comparing each market segment's needs and wants with the strengths and weaknesses of the businesses in the matrix. Each segment of the market places a different value or priority on the

Competitive factor	Business #1	Business #2	Business #3	Business #4	Business #5
Price	3	1	2	4	3
Quality	3	3	2	3	2
Selection	4	4	3	3	4
Promotion	3	4	2	4	2
Services	4	5	2	3	4
Customer service/ sales personnel	3	3	1	3	3
Facilities/ atmosphere	3	5	2	2	3
Location	3	4	2	2	3

Rating of the business on this factor ———→

Figure 4-2. Competitive matrix reflecting the rating of existing businesses.

various dimensions of the marketing mix. A segment comprising lower-income families operating on a limited budget may place a premium on low prices, access to public transportation, in-house credit, and brands that offer a warranty. A market segment comprising upper-income, double-wage-earning couples without children may be interested in

Competitive factor	Business #1	Business #2	Business #3	Business #4	Business #5
Price (importance 3)	3 x 3 = 9	★ 1 x 3 = 3	★ 2 x 3 = 6	4 x 3 = 12	3 x 3 = 9
Quality (importance 5)	★ 3 x 5 = 15	★ 3 x 5 = 15	★ 2 x 5 = 10	★ 3 x 5 = 15	★ 2 x 5 = 10
Selection (importance 3)	4 x 3 = 12	4 x 3 = 12	3 x 3 = 9	3 x 3 = 9	4 x 3 = 12
Promotion (importance 2)	3 x 2 = 6	4 x 2 = 8	2 x 2 = 4	4 x 2 = 8	2 x 2 = 4
Services (importance 5)	★ 4 x 5 = 20	5 x 5 = 25	★ 2 x 5 = 10	★ 3 x 5 = 15	★ 4 x 5 = 20
Customer service/ sales personnel (importance 5)	★ 3 x 5 = 15	★ 3 x 5 = 15	★ 1 x 5 = 5	★ 3 x 5 = 15	★ 3 x 5 = 15
Facilities/ atmosphere (importance 4)	★ 3 x 4 = 12	5 x 4 = 20	★ 2 x 4 = 8	★ 2 x 4 = 8	★ 3 x 4 = 12
Location (importance 2)	3 x 2 = 6	4 x 2 = 8	2 x 2 = 4	2 x 2 = 4	3 x 2 = 6
Relative strength for this segment	95	106	56	86	88

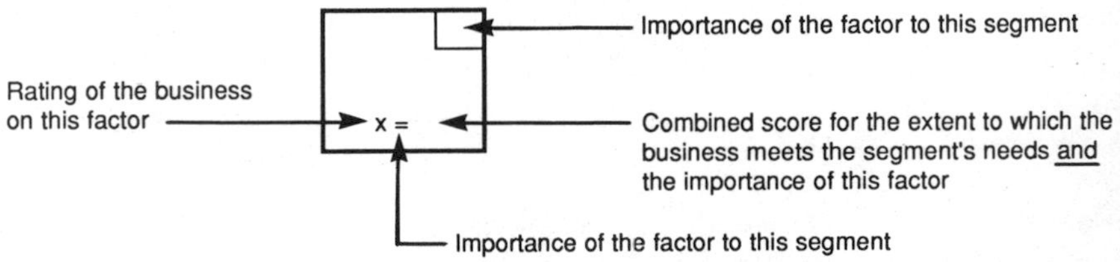

Importance of the factor to this segment

Rating of the business on this factor ──► x = ◄── Combined score for the extent to which the business meets the segment's needs and the importance of this factor

Importance of the factor to this segment

★ Indicates that a "gap" exists between what this business offers and what this segment wants.

Figure 4-3. Competitive matrix reflecting "gaps" in the marketplace.

exclusive brands, knowledgeable salespeople, delivery services, evening hours, and the opportunity to place phone orders. You should rate the relative importance of each dimension of the marketing mix on a 1 to 5 scale for each segment.

Now that you have rated each business in terms of its market offering or mix, you can compare the market's preferences and priorities one segment at a time. With this data, you can determine if "gaps" exist between what consumers desire and what the existing businesses offer. The gaps represent opportunities. They represent customers in search of a business. For example, if you were investigating the retail seafood market, you might find a segment that places a premium on phone orders, that wants to use their VISA cards, have their fish filleted, and get delivery service, and is not very price-sensitive. You would then check the matrix to see if any existing business offers the people in this segment what they are looking for.

If no business in the matrix offers these services, this indicates a possible area for starting a business with a competitive advantage for that particular segment. A comparison of each segment's preferences with the matrix may reveal several other gaps or opportunities. This is similar to Step 1 in Chapter 2. It needs to be followed by Step 2 (determining whether you can develop the capability to be better than your competitors and meet the segment's needs) and Step 3 (estimating the level of profitability and the return on investment before you select the segment you are going to use as the target for your business). If (1) a sufficiently large need is evident and competition does not appear able to serve it, (2) you believe you can provide the segment what it wants, and (3) you can generate a level of profit to meet your return-on-investment objective, then this is where you need to focus your attention.

Identifying Your Prospective Customers

At this point you should be able to develop a "customer profile" that describes specifically the nature of the people in your target market. The overall market is like a target. Your target market is the bull's-eye. Remember, no business can be all things to all the people. You should concentrate your attention on being the best to the people in your target market.

If you cannot provide a customer profile of your target market in terms of who they are, where they live, whether they are white collar versus blue collar, what they do with their time and money, as well as their preferences for products, services, and brands, then you will not be able to tailor your marketing mix to their specific needs, interests, wants, desires, and behavioral patterns.

Big businesses and a number of small businesses try the "shotgun" approach to creating customers. They try to be or do too many different things for too many different people. They are not very successful because their marketing mixes are compromises. They try to have something for everyone rather than offer the best for a few. When a business treats the market in general terms as if everyone is alike, few people get exactly what they want. The rest of the people remain customers in search of a business. This is also true when a business tries to serve a combination of segments with a single marketing mix.

You need to use the "rifle" approach where you select a specific market segment (bull's-eye) and offer customers exactly what they are looking for. This is the formula for creating and maintaining customers for a profit. Effective marketing boils down to using the rifle approach to create and maintain customers who are part of a specific market segment. This process is similar to how hunters go after big game. Businesses try to appeal to a group of people by offering a marketing mix that is tailored to that group's unique interests. Successful hunters identify a certain type of animal to go after, study its unique behavioral patterns, and develop an approach to shoot it.

The distinction should be made between businesses and hunters. Businesses don't want to kill their customers. They want them to come back time and time again. They also want customers to encourage their own friends and associates to try the businesses. Ironically, many hunters have replaced their rifles with cameras. They have realized that their hunting will continue only as long as they have animals to "shoot" with their cameras.

Let's stay with the business-hunter-photographer analogy a little longer. The similarities provide additional insight into how a new business can create and maintain customers for a profit.

A new business will be successful to the extent its manager is able to identify a group of customers in search of a business, know the group's unique characteristics, and tailor its marketing mix to that uniqueness. The most successful hunters-photographers try to know as much as possible about their target before they initiate the hunt. They try to learn how big it is, how it moves, if it lives alone or in groups, and if it has keen senses of smell, sight, and hearing. The more the hunter-photographer knows about the target, the higher the probability of a successful expedition. The same applies to a new business's ability to create and maintain customers.

Unfortunately, it may be more difficult for you to learn about the nature of your target market(s) than for hunters to learn about their prey. A significant part of animal behavior is the result of instinct. Consumers can be more elusive because most of their behavior is learned. People are more complex. Their attitudes are the product of many factors, and their behavior is influenced by numerous forces.

A new business needs to be tailored to the unique nature of the market segment(s) that will be its target market(s). There are five useful ways to help identify the nature of the people who constitute your target market: Demographic, geographic, psychographic, benefit, and usage factors will help you formulate a customer profile, discussed later in this chapter.

Demographic Factors. This set of factors is fairly easy to measure. It includes age, sex, level of income, occupation, nationality, educational level, race, religion, and stage of family life cycle (single, married, married with preschool children, retired, etc.). This type of information is readily available for most cities and counties in the United States. If you are trying to determine which geographic areas may offer the best opportunities, then demographic analysis may be beneficial. This approach uses census data that is available from the *County and City Data Book*, published by the U.S. Department of Commerce, and *The Survey of Buying Power Data Service*, published by Sales and Marketing Management. The census of population is done every 10 years by the Bureau of the Census. The Bureau of the Census also publishes the *Statistical Abstract of the United States*, which provides an annual summary of population, prices, income, housing, etc. The *Editor and Publisher Market Guide* and *Metro Insights* are also useful.

These databases are frequently used by marketers when they are trying to locate new markets. Ray Kroc referred to the *Editor and Publisher Market Guide* so often that he kept a copy of it in his personal jet. *Metro Insights* is published each year by Data Resources. It provides econometric profits and forecasts for the top 100 urban areas in the United States. Your local library may have these sources. If not, check with the reference librarian at the nearest university.

The databases will enable you to put together a multidimensional profile of the area you want to research. Once you have developed a profile for each area, it will be possible to compare the areas under consideration to determine which ones have the most potential.

The *County and City Data Book* contains the following types of information on each city:

- Number of people employed in manufacturing, wholesale and retail jobs, professional services, and government, and number who are self-employed.
- Average value of a household.
- Average age of a household.

- Percentage of female householders with husband present.
- Number enrolled in elementary schools.
- Number enrolled in high schools.
- Number of people with a college education.
- Number of people with a high school education.
- Percentage of population that has moved within the area, within the state, and out-of-state or to another country.
- Percentage of population in each race.
- Maps showing county lines within the state and the location of major cities.

The July issue of *Sales and Marketing Management Magazine* each year provides the following information for regions, states, counties, and cities:

- Population for area.
- Percentage of U.S. population residing in that metropolitan area, county, or city.
- Median age of the population for that area, and percentage of population by age group.
- Number of households, and the average number of people in the household units.
- Total retail sales and sales volume for various businesses, including food stores, eating places, general merchandise stores, furniture and appliance stores, and drugstores.
- Effective buying income for that area. This figure is equivalent to the after-tax income or level of affluence.
- Buying power index, which converts the effective buying income, total population, and total retail sales into the area's "ability to buy" index.
- Computation of the median household effective buying income.
- Percentage of households with incomes of less than $10,000; $10,000 to $20,000; $20,000 to $35,000; $35,000 to $50,000; and over $50,000.

The *Survey of Buying Power Data Service* reference book is published each year. It contains the information available in the July issue of *Sales and Marketing Management Magazine*, plus the following:

- Computation of the buying power index for economy priced, moderate priced, and premium priced products for each area by breaking the population into income groups of less than $15,000; $15,000 to $35,000; and over $35,000.
- A ranking of cities in the United States by effective buying income.
- Population and population density.
- Percentage change in population.
- Population by age and sex.
- Households by age of householder and number of persons per household.
- Number of households per effective buying index group.
- Median household effective buying income.
- Per capita effective buying income.
- Sales for certain types of stores.
- Projections of retail sales, population changes, number of households, the buying power index, effective buyer income, etc., for each region, state, and county.

The *Editor and Publisher Market Guide* provides a profile on more than 1500 cities and communities in the United States and Canada where a daily newspaper is published. The following information is included in each profile:

- Kinds of industries.
- Largest shopping centers.
- Number of retail stores by category, including chain stores.
- Sales by category of stores.
- Disposable personal income.
- Population estimates.
- Number of passenger autos.
- Newspaper circulation.
- Number of stores per category.

Numerous other sources of demographic information for a market may also be available from each city's planning department, the respective state's department of commerce, the local chamber of commerce, area banks, business schools at neighboring universities, and the U.S.

Small Business Administration. Local newspapers often have a wealth of information about their communities.

Geographic Factors.   People can also be described in terms of where they live. Geographic factors include whether people live in (1) the north vs. the south, (2) an urban, suburban, or rural area, (3) a small town vs. a large city, (4) a warm vs. a cold climate, or (5) tropical vs. arid conditions.

Psychographic Factors.   These factors pertain to people's "lifestyles." Attention is directed to whether they are (1) outgoing vs. withdrawn, (2) confident and willing to try new things vs. risk-averse and satisfied with the status quo, or (3) energetic and athletic vs. reserved and homebodies. Psychographic factors provide insight into people's interests, attitudes, and propensities to behave in a particular manner.

Benefit Factors.   People buy products and services for various reasons. Restaurants provide a good example. People may go to a restaurant for the food it offers; but they may also go there because they like the cocktails, the bartender, the atmosphere, the waiters and waitresses, and the opportunity to meet people and to be seen. Years ago, restaurants located near wealthy neighborhoods did good business on Thursday nights. On Thursday nights, the maids had their nights off. This example illustrates how a benefit factor (not wanting to cook and clean the dishes) and a demographic factor (high-level income) produced a certain type of behavior by a specific segment of the market.

Benefit analysis applies to movie theaters as well. Most teenagers do not go to see a movie. They go to meet their friends and to check out the other teenagers. Adults go to health clubs for numerous reasons, not just to be more fit. Many people join spas because it is a socially acceptable way to check out people of the opposite sex who are wearing next to nothing.

Benefit analysis is important to the development of the marketing mix. If you are not in tune with what people in your target market are looking for, you will not be in a position to satisfy their needs. Remember, you are not in business to sell products and services, you are in business to provide satisfaction. Revlon and Disney exemplify this concept. Revlon's approach to the market can be paraphrased, "We may make cosmetics, but we offer customers hope!" Disney management constantly reminds its employees that Disney is not in the amusement park business. It is in the business of "making people happy."

Usage Factors.   People who are involved in marketing have a saying, "If you can't sell all the people something, then sell a lot to some of the people." People can be classified into (1) non-, (2) light, (3) medium, and (4) heavy user categories.

If you have a sales goal of $120,000 for your first year of operation and your product sells for $50, then there are various ways to reach your sales goal. You can try to sell one product to 2400 people. Conversely, you could try to find one person to buy 2400 items. The last scenario is fairly unlikely, but it does illustrate the value of usage-rate analysis. Some businesses benefit from the 80/20 rule. In these businesses, 80 percent of total sales come from 20 percent of the customers. Businesses obviously need to pay particular attention to the 20 percent. They also want to know where they can find more people like them.

Usage-rate analysis has yielded some interesting information. Years ago, a major brewery studied beer consumption. Its research classified people according to how many "12-ounce equivalents" (the size of a beer can) people consumed on a daily basis. People were classified as nonconsumers, light consumers, medium consumers, or heavy consumers. However, the brewery found that it needed to create a fifth category: the "super-heavies." The market study revealed that the number of people who consumed at least twenty-four 12-ounce equivalents a day was large enough for the group to be considered a separate segment.

People in the auto business also pay attention to usage rates. Auto dealers are particularly interested in how often people trade in their cars. Tire dealers are interested in how many miles people drive each year and how often they replace their tires. Car washes, muffler shops, and gas stations also want to know about the different usage categories of customers.

Restaurants illustrate the value of the usage-rate classification system as a way of identifying customers. As a restaurateur, your marketing mix would be very different if you were going after people who live in one particular neighborhood, who dine out three times a week, and who are loyal to one restaurant. A different marketing mix would be used if the target market you were trying to attract consisted of tourists or conventioneers who might be in that town only once in their lifetimes.

Consumer loyalty represents another dimension for usage-rate analysis. Consumers vary in their loyalty to particular businesses and specific brands. Some people will not even try a competitive brand or business. Other people are willing to shop around and compare product and service offerings.

Consumers can be classified as having low, medium, or high levels of loyalty. Anyone who is considering starting a business should investigate the extent to which consumers are loyal to businesses already in the market. Highly loyal customers tend to not pay attention to the competitions' advertisements and usually are unwilling to try new stores or brands. If your market analysis reveals that a large percentage of the people in the market have a low level of loyalty, then this means there are customers still in search of a business.

Putting Together the "Customer Profile"

The preceding discussion of ways consumers can be classified or described indicates the multidimensional nature of people in the marketplace. People who are contemplating starting a business frequently say, "Wouldn't it be a lot easier if all consumers were alike?" It would be easier to tailor your offering to the market if John Smith's interests were the same as Susan Jones' interests. However, if everyone wanted the same thing, then a few large businesses would dominate the marketplace. Their economies of scale would give them a cost advantage that would enable them to undercut most small businesses.

The beauty of our marketplace is that consumers are multidimensional. Instead of one tremendous homogeneous market, we have thousands of heterogeneous segments. Within each segment, there are enough similarities of interests among consumers for a business to tailor its offerings to meet their needs. The differences in people may make it more difficult to identify and understand them. But their differences are the reason why so many opportunities exist today for new businesses. As people's needs change and their desire to express their individuality increases, opportunities for new ventures also increase.

A new business must direct its market offering to one or more segments of the population in which customers are in search of a business. As noted earlier, the rifle approach will be effective only if you can clearly identify the specific target market you will be trying to satisfy. Market-analysis and market-segment selection require that you be able to compile a customer profile which describes the unique nature of your target market.

The customer profile plays an essential role in your marketing effort. If you can describe the people you are trying to satisfy, then you will be in a better position to develop a marketing mix that is tailored to their particular needs. The customer profile can be viewed as a tapestry woven with numerous strands of thread. The customer profile attempts to identify the key dimensions (threads) and how they are interrelated (woven) to constitute the unique nature of that target market (tapestry).

The customer profile represents the "bull's-eye" of your target market. The more you understand what the people in the target market value in life, how they spend their time, how they spend their money, and what they want but don't have enough of, the more likely you will be to meet their needs. If you understand their lifestyles, then you will have an idea about what goods and services they need, how often they use certain products and services, and whether they are loyal to one store or brand. You will also gain insight into how much disposable income they have and whether they are price-sensitive. If you know when they drive to work and what radio stations they listen to, then you will be in a better position to design radio spots that are in tune with their interests, and you will air them at a time when they are listening.

The same logic also applies to locating your business or finding ways to distribute your product or services. If you are going after one particular segment of parents, as was the case with Early Childhood Development Centers described in Chapter 3, then you will want to know where they live so your location will be within a five-minute drive of your target market. However, if you plan to manufacture a line of items for people throughout the United States, then you may choose a location that is close to distribution facilities.

The customer profile should be as specific as possible. When someone asks you to whom you will be targeting your marketing efforts, you will need to have something more specific than, "Anyone who will buy my products and services." The following customer profile for a clothing boutique may serve as an example of an attempt to identify a specific target market:

> Cachet Fashions International is targeted to professional women between the ages of 35 and 55 who earn at least $70,000 per year, who pay at least $400 for a dress and $150 for shoes for everyday use and $1250 or more for an outfit for special occasions, who spend at least $10,000 per year on clothes, who are style conscious yet maintain traditional values, who are moderately loyal to certain brands yet willing to try a new brand, who want their clothes to be tailored to flatter their figures, who entertain regularly, who drive a car less than three years old that cost at least $30,000, who live in a house or condominium valued in excess of $450,000, who take at least three vacations per year, with one or more being outside the continental United States, who have their own personal credit cards with at least a $5000 limit per card, who have at least $15,000 in jewelry, who subscribe to magazines such as *Harper's Bazaar, Town & Country, Architectural Digest*, and *Forbes*, and who live or work within a 60-mile radius of Manhattan.

This customer profile includes many of the factors described earlier. It illustrates that knowing the specifics of the target market will enable a business to tailor its marketing mix to the unique needs, interests, and behavioral patterns of its target market.

A business may have more than one target market. Cachet's customer profile was for women in a certain age range with a certain income who lived in a certain area. This isn't to say that Cachet would be unwilling to sell its products to someone less than 35 who is on vacation or on a business trip in Manhattan or who doesn't have a full-time job. Most successful businesses also have secondary target markets. Each of these target markets will have a corresponding customer profile.

A secondary target market may also affect the business's marketing mix. If Cachet's secondary target market consists of women who may be traveling to Manhattan on a business trip or on a weekend vacation to catch the latest Broadway show, then Cachet will have to expand its advertising to include magazines these people may read. Cachet will also need to have a location that is highly visible and convenient to its secondary target market.

A note of caution would be appropriate here. It is usually better for a new business to concentrate on serving one market well rather than trying to have something for everybody. In Cachet's case, it would be better to concentrate 80 percent of its sales on its primary target market and 20 percent on tourists than to try to split its mix right down the middle. The greater the differences between your primary and secondary market, the more you should consider having two separate businesses, each to cater to the unique needs of each respective target market. The rifle approach works best if you are shooting at a target with only one bull's-eye.

5

Product-Service Strategy and Price Strategy

Now that you have analyzed the market, determined the strengths and weaknesses of the existing businesses, and identified your target market, you are in a position to develop your marketing mix. The marketing mix represents your way of creating and maintaining customers for a profit. Your business's marketing mix reflects what you plan to have for a competitive advantage and how you will be able to offer greater satisfaction to your target market than any other business.

One of the basic principles for business success is, "To succeed, you must be better than your competition. To be better, you must be different." Your marketing mix must be better in areas your target market values. Being different does not automatically mean you will be better. You may have exclusive rights to distribute a line of Nehru coats that were popular decades ago. But if you are located in a small, out-of-the-way town, don't be surprised if the market does not consider your line of clothes to be better than your competitors' lines.

Your market offering is better only if your target market considers it to be better. Better means that your target market values it and is willing to pay for it. For example, the owners of La Tour Eiffel may claim it to be the best French restaurant in Chicago. The owner may base this claim on the head chef's credentials and his commitment to using only the finest ingredients. Professional accomplishments and expensive ingredients may affect the taste of the food, but it will be the expectations and preferences of the people in the target market that determine whether they consider it to be the best. This is why it is so important that you be in tune with the people in your target market and that you try to see the world through their eyes.

New businesses must be tailored to the needs, desires, interests, preferences, and behaviors of their target markets. Your target market is the judge and the jury when your business goes on trial in the marketplace. You may believe you have the lowest prices in town, but if your target market is price-sensitive and believes you are not the lowest, then they will go somewhere else. The same applies to your location and the other components of your market offering. If you believe that your business is conveniently located, but your target market considers it to be out of the way, they will take their business elsewhere.

Your marketing mix represents the bullet your business fires at the target market. You need to be sure the bullet hits your target market's bull's-eye. Again, your marketing mix constitutes your strategy for developing a competitive advantage and your game plan for creating and maintaining customers for a profit.

The marketing mix is comprised of four components, which are known as the "4 P's." These components are the product-service strategy, price strategy, promotional strategy, and physical distribution strategy.

Product-Service Strategy

Each component of the marketing mix plays an integral role in your effort to create and maintain customers. Product-service strategy may play the most significant role of the 4 P's. Businesses are usually described in terms of the kind of goods and services they offer the marketplace. Pricing, advertising, and physical distribution factors also are important. However, if the goods and services you offer are not what people in your target market desire and are willing to buy, then it will not matter how low your prices are, how catchy your advertising may be, or if you operate out of a convenient location.

The development of your product-service strategy begins with identifying which products and services to offer. The competitive matrix will be helpful here. Market analysis may indicate that customers in your target market are still searching for colors, sizes, or types of that particular product. The matrix may also indicate that your target market is looking for a specific brand that is not available in your geographic territory.

The product-service mix can be described in terms of its breadth and depth. Breadth refers to how many different brands you offer. A business with a broad product mix offers a variety of brands. The depth of the product line refers to the number of models offered for each brand.

The broader and deeper your product mix, the greater the selection for your target market. A note of caution may be appropriate here. If you offer the wrong brands, it may not matter how many models you carry in stock. This is why it is important to determine if your target market is brand conscious and brand-loyal.

Retail sporting goods stores provide an example of having a broad and deep product mix. Most sporting goods stores carry at least six different brands of shoes and at least five models for each brand. A few decades ago, this was not the case. Everyone wore "regular" white tennis shoes. Now there are low-cut, high-cut, pastel-colored, zebra-patterned, hard court, soft court, exercise, jogging, and aerobic shoes.

If market analysis indicates a trend whereby people want to have a different athletic shoe for each sport, then sporting goods stores will need to have the breadth and depth of product mix to provide a competitive advantage. Henry Ford's product strategy for his Model T, based on the premise, "You can have your car in any color as long as it is black," no longer applies to automobiles and it doesn't apply to most other products in today's Baskin-Robbins, 31-flavors marketplace.

The product-service strategy also involves the services you plan to offer your target market. The United States has become a service economy. Even though service businesses sell labor, the process of developing a "service" strategy is not very different from the process of developing a product strategy. The primary difference between products and services is that, in many cases, potential customers may be able to do the services for themselves. Residential real estate sales, moving household furnishings, landscaping, hair styling, bookkeeping, exercise activities, and house painting businesses compete not only against other businesses but against consumers who may be able to provide the services for themselves if they find it worthwhile.

Service businesses succeed to the extent they are able to provide their services better, quicker, in a more convenient way, or in a less expensive manner than their competition or their customers could. If a service business does not have a competitive advantage, then why should consumers give it their money?

Most businesses that sell products also provide various services. The competitive matrix may indicate that customers are in search of a business that will: (1) provide a delivery service, (2) take phone orders, (3) have knowledgeable salespeople, (4) do special orders, (5) provide a warranty or a money-back refund, (6) accept credit cards, or (7) provide advice on how to use the products.

When you are trying to decide which products to carry, keep in mind the saying, "You want to offer products that don't come back, and to offer them to people who do." The more that you offer what the people in your target market want, the higher the probability they will be loyal to your business. This is important, because the higher the level of customer satisfaction and loyalty, the less likely the customers will be to try other businesses or to be influenced by your competitors' advertisements.

Everybody who is contemplating going into business needs to remember that they are not in the business of selling products or services. They need to be in the business of providing satisfaction. If you plan to open a business that sells products, you may find that your greatest competitive advantage may be in the services you offer with your products. Most existing businesses do a poor job when it comes to providing customer service. Their salespeople resemble the living dead. They know little about the products they stock. More often than not, customers feel like calling in the Civil Air Patrol to help find someone to take their money.

If you will be offering the same products as everyone else, at comparable prices, and in a location no better than your competitors', then you will have to offer your target market some reason to do business with you. The service part of your product-service strategy may make the difference. It could be your competitive advantage.

Even if you offer the best products, prices, and location, guard yourself against the tendency to become complacent. After all, when the next person analyzes the market to identify an area of business opportunity, your business may be rated low on the customer service dimension of the competitive matrix. You will be laying out the welcome mat for additional competition.

It should be apparent that a business's product-service strategy cannot be viewed in isolation. It is an integral part of the marketing mix. Your product-service strategy needs to be consistent with the other three P's of the marketing mix. In some situations, your product-service offering may be your competitive advantage; in other cases, it may be less significant. Most businesses can be classified according to the extent their target markets place a premium on the product-service offering. Accordingly, businesses can be classified into the specialty, shopping, convenience, or impulse category.

Product-Service Classifications

Specialty Items. A specialty business offers a brand that is valued by the target market. This type of business may have exclusive rights to distribute a brand in a geographic area. In a specialty business, consumers are not very price-sensitive, less likely to be influenced by advertisements by competitors, and willing to go out of their way to buy that particular brand, product, or service. This situation was portrayed in two advertisements years ago. Camel cigarettes had an ad with a picture of a man's shoe with a hole in the bottom. The caption read, "I'd walk a mile for a Camel." The other ad was by Schlitz Brewery. Schlitz had the slogan, "When you're out of Schlitz, you're out of beer!" Both of these companies tried to project the image that they offered specialty items. If your market analysis indicates that the target market has a strong preference for a specific brand, product, or service that is not available in your trading area, then this may represent the best opportunity for you to develop a competitive advantage.

The specialty type of business often involves customizing your product-service offering to the needs of your potential customers. Years ago, an individual who was an avid pizza consumer was standing at the order counter of his favorite pizza restaurant. When he noticed one of his colleagues at the pickup counter, he asked him if he went to any other restaurant in the area for pizza. His friend stated that he goes to Guido's Pizzeria when he is across town because they serve "white" pizza. The friend said he frequently preferred white pizza because it did not have as much tomato paste. White pizza did not upset his stomach as much as traditional red pizza. The first person then said he would have to give Guido's "white" pizza a try. The chef must have overheard the conversation because he came out and said, "If you want white pizza, I'll make you white pizza!"

The chef at the pizza restaurant illustrated the points: (1) the customer is always right, (2) you need to offer what the customer wants to buy, not what you want to sell, and (3) you are in the business of providing satisfaction, not selling products and services. You must be willing and able to tailor your products and services to your target market. You should not expect your target market to change its wants and behavior to what you want to sell.

Shopping Items.   Numerous goods and services are considered to be shopping items by certain segments of the market. Something is considered a shopping item if consumers compare its price and quality. Consumers of shopping items "shop" around and compare the prices and attributes of numerous brands. They may prefer one brand to another, but they look at the "value" of the item. Value is the combination of price and quality. People who are comparing shopping items are looking for a good deal. They may prefer the General Electric brand over the Panasonic brand, but if the Panasonic item is priced less than the GE item, the consumer may buy the Panasonic product. Brands may still be a factor in shopping items, but brand loyalty is not as strong as it is with specialty items.

Quite a few products and services are shopping items. A large percentage of Americans do comparison shopping. They are willing to check three or more stores to find the best value. This is why furniture stores are located near other furniture stores. Most people want to see what is available before they buy the product. The same principle applies to car dealerships and clothing stores. Some restaurants that are located in "restaurant rows" display their menus at their entrances to permit potential customers to check them out.

If your market analysis indicates that existing businesses offer a fairly wide selection of products or services but that their prices are higher than they should be, then this may represent an opportunity for you to create a competitive advantage by matching their product-service offering but offering lower prices. This may be effective if you have a reasonable location and if your competitors don't retaliate by lowering their prices. This is why it is advisable that you have numerous competitive advantages when you develop your marketing mix.

Convenience Items. The brand of a product went from being very important in the specialty business to being moderately important in the shopping-type business where selection and value were the key elements. Convenience items reflect even less concern by consumers for a particular brand, a particular size, or even a particular price. Some consumers place a premium on how easy it is to purchase certain items.

In the last two decades, the United States has experienced a "convenience" revolution. People prefer not to go out of their way or not to get out of their cars. There used to be a gas station on every corner. Now there is a convenience store on every corner. Banks, restaurants, laundries, drugstores, and liquor stores have selected locations near their target markets. They have also built drive-in windows to make it easier for their customers to do business. Other businesses offer delivery service so the customer doesn't even need to get into the car. Malls represent large-scale convenience stores. Like their predecessor, the large department store, they try to offer one-stop shopping.

The key ingredient to a convenience item is just what its name implies: it must be convenient to the target market. Most convenience businesses are built on the premise that their consumers frequently place convenience ahead of brand loyalty and price consciousness. The typical neighborhood convenience store will not carry all the top brands nor will it offer a broad and deep product selection. Instead, it will stock one or two brands in one or two sizes. Convenience stores try to carry basic items that people run out of, including bread, milk, gasoline, beer, cigarettes, and film. In a sense, convenience stores can be viewed as "emergency" stores. When people run out of something before they expected to, they want to get it in a hurry. This is why the location, facility, and hours may be the most important parts of a convenience business. The "emergency" nature of convenience items explains why convenience stores can get away with charging higher prices.

The lack of product selection and higher prices are the price people pay for convenience. People are less particular about the brand and price when they are in a hurry. Convenience businesses tailor their marketing mixes to certain target markets. People who are brand-loyal tend to drive farther to get their favorite brand. People who are price-conscious are willing to shop where they can get lower prices, even if it takes them more time.

Convenience stores, drive-in windows, delivery services, vending machines, and shop-by-phone businesses are a sign of the times. The convenience approach to business is suited to people in target markets who have disposable income and who place a premium on the value of their time.

Impulse Items.   The best way to describe an impulse item is that the consumer did not plan to buy it. Impulse items do not appear on people's shopping lists. They tend to be spur-of-the-moment purchases. Food represents the best example of an impulse item. Small food booths at shopping malls make most of their money from people who did not go to the mall to buy food. The same applies to the sale of candy at drugstores and grocery stores. Most people did not go there to buy candy. A large portion of sales by ice cream and yogurt shops located on major thoroughfares can also be attributed to impulse purchases.

Most impulse purchases are the product of emotions rather than necessity. Most of the products and services that can be classified as impulse items must be located and displayed in such a way that it is easy for the potential consumer to see and purchase them. In a sense, people in the impulse business make their living by getting customers for other businesses who are looking for other products and services to spend a moment of their time and some of their money on impulse items. Product-service strategy is important, but the location, visibility, and display of impulse items may be just as important.

Matching Your Product-Service Strategy to Your Target Market

Business success is directly related to the extent the product-service offering is tailored to the target market's unique interests. The four categories of product-service offering provide a means for describing how particular your target market may be about products and services.

You need to recognize that a shopping item to one person may be a convenience item to another person and an impulse item to a third person. Automobiles are shopping items for most people. People tend to compare models, prices, financing, and warranties before they make a decision. This process could involve all members of the family and take months before the final decision is made. However, some people will only buy one particular brand, at one particular dealer, and from one particular salesperson. A few people approach buying an automobile as if it were a convenience or even an impulse item. The differences in what people look for in products and services represent opportunities for new businesses.

Pricing Strategy

Your pricing strategy will depend on numerous factors. Prices will need to reflect the target market you select, the nature and extent of competition, the strength of your location, your cost structure, and the type of goods and services you will offer. There may be as many approaches to pricing as there are factors that affect a business's pricing strategy.

The Standard Markup Approach

Quite a few businesses use the standard markup or "cost-based" approach to setting their prices. The standard markup means that a retailer will base its price for an item on what the retailer paid for it plus a percentage of that cost. The percentage of cost added to the cost is what is referred to as the markup. The standard markup formula is:

$$\text{Retail price} = \text{cost} + \text{markup}$$

The percentage of markup may be suggested by your suppliers or it could be based on other cost-related factors.

Two examples illustrate the standard markup approach. Many retailers use a customary markup of 100 percent of cost. The owner of a wine and cheese shop buys a bottle of imported French wine for $6, then places a price of $12 on that bottle. The 100 percent markup is easy to figure. Your price to your customers will be twice what you paid for it.

Service businesses frequently use the standard markup approach. One CPA firm's hourly rate is three times what it pays the accountants who will be doing the work. The logic behind their pricing strategy is that the price for their services has to cover three equal components. The first component is what the CPA firm has to pay the accountants for the work they actually do. The second component is for the fringe benefits, social security payments, training time, and the time the accountants are in their offices between clients. The second component also includes office rent, insurance, clerical assistance, and the depreciation of equipment. This component represents the "overhead" of the business. The third component is to help cover the salaries of senior managers who coordinate the firm's operations and to generate a reasonable profit.

The standard markup approach is fairly common in certain types of businesses. If you are starting a certain type of business and want to have an idea of what is the average markup, you can check trade data or *Robert Morris Associates, Inc.'s Annual Statement Studies* to get the average markup figure. Trade data frequently reports the gross margin as a percentage of sales. The gross margin is the result of subtracting the cost of goods sold from sales. If trade data indicates that gross margin is 40 percent of sales, then you know that the cost of goods must be 60 percent of sales. If an item sells for $10, then the business had to pay $6 for it. The gross margin represents the markup of $4 on a cost of $6 per unit. If gross margin is 40 percent of sales, then the markup on cost is 66 percent of cost.

The standard markup method has two major shortcomings. It fails to take into consideration the unique nature of the market or competition. The standard markup approach is based on costs rather than market conditions. It also assumes that your competition uses the same approach and that your customers are willing to buy your products or services at those prices.

The Match-the-Market Approach

This approach resembles the standard markup approach. Businesses that compete against one another may offer their products-services at comparable prices. If they use a standard markup and have comparable products or services, then their prices will be fairly close to one another.

The situation may arise where one or two of the businesses may decide to lower the markup percentage to attract additional customers. Conversely, owners may think that customers are not price-sensitive, and then raise the markup to increase profits. Some or all of the other competitors may then "match" the new prices. After a period of time and changes, prices may reflect what one or two businesses think prices should be rather than the standard markup percentage.

New businesses frequently choose the matching strategy. Consumers have already demonstrated their willingness to buy goods and services at these prices, so new businesses match their competitors' prices. This

approach has numerous drawbacks. The primary drawback is that if
you have a competitive advantage that your target market values, you
should be able to charge higher prices. The match-the-market approach
is a "play it safe approach" that fails to consider your unique strengths.

The Market-Based Approach to Pricing

With this approach numerous factors are taken into account. You begin
by analyzing the nature of the target market and determining if potential customers prefer a certain brand, if they have disposable income, if
they are price-sensitive, how often they buy your types of products or
services, and whether they consider the item to be in the specialty, shopping, convenience, or impulse category.

Using this approach you pay particular attention to the competitive
matrix for the target market. The number of businesses in the market
and the extent to which those businesses meet your target market's
needs will affect your price strategy. If the matrix indicates that numerous businesses already offer a good selection of products, brands, or
services, have reasonable prices, and are conveniently located, then it
may not be advisable to set your prices higher than your competitors'.
You may be better off matching your competitors' prices or offering
lower prices to entice their customers to try your business.

The Market-Penetration Approach to Pricing

If the target market is price-sensitive, then you may consider a "market-
penetration" pricing strategy. This strategy gets its name because you
are trying to enter the market by diverting customers to your business
or getting people who have not bought before to buy because the lower
prices have greater appeal. The penetration approach works best when
existing businesses have been taking advantage of the market by charging higher-than-appropriate prices. If you enter the market and try to
divert your competition's customers to your business, do not be surprised if they lower their prices to match or beat your prices.

Most established businesses prefer not to compete on the basis of
price. They want to avoid price wars, if at all possible. After all, if prices
go up, new competition may enter the market. If prices go too low,
there may not be enough gross margin to cover operating expenses and
generate profits.

Penetration may be a viable pricing strategy for a new business if its cost structure is considerably lower than the existing businesses' cost structure. K-mart used this strategy when it entered the retail market. It was able to offer lower prices than Sears because it located its stores on the outskirts of cities where rent rates were much lower. K-mart's management believed that if it offered brand names at lower prices, then consumers would be willing to drive a little farther to save money.

You may be able to attract other businesses' customers with lower prices if the other 3 P's of the marketing mix are comparable. If your location is too far out of the way, then you will probably have to lower your prices even more to make it worthwhile for people to travel farther to buy your goods and services. If your prices are just a few cents lower than more conveniently located businesses, then you had better not hold your breath while waiting for customers to switch to your business.

The Skimming Approach to Pricing

If your review of the competitive matrix indicates that customers are still in search of a business, then you may have an opportunity to set higher prices. If you have the exclusive distribution rights for a revolutionary new product or a popular brand that the market has been anxiously waiting for, then you may have some latitude in setting prices. You may consider a "skimming" strategy. When people want something, they are usually willing to pay more for it. By charging higher prices, you are going after the group of people in your target market who are willing to pay for something that is new or prestigious. The same applies to your location. If you offer a convenience type of product or service and are located much closer to your target market than any other business, then your price may reflect your competitive advantage.

The skimming approach to pricing has four possible drawbacks. First, it assumes that your business is better than any other. Second, it assumes that your market is willing to pay more. Third, higher prices means that fewer people will be able to pay for the items. Fourth, the higher the prices, the greater the likelihood that other businesses will enter the market to lure your customers by offering lower prices.

If you have a competitive advantage, then you should be able to set higher prices. Your review of the target market and the probability of competitive retaliation will give you an idea about how much higher your prices can be as well as how long they can be higher.

Both the penetration and skimming strategies require judgment. Neither strategy will assure success. Nevertheless, they may be more appropriate than the other strategies that ignore the nature of the market.

Additional Pricing Guidelines

Each of the preceding approaches provides a general basis for pricing products and services. Your pricing strategy also needs to address sales discounts and seasonality.

You will need to decide whether you will discount your prices for various situations. The most common type of discount is to put your products or services "on sale." You may lower your prices temporarily for certain items to attract new customers, to have your existing customers buy more, to sell inventory that has been building up, or to raise cash to meet pressing financial obligations.

Before you put anything on sale, you need to answer three questions: (1) Which items will attract customer interest? (2) How much of a discount will I need to offer to attract customers? and (3) How long should the items be on sale?

The answers to these questions will depend on the uniqueness of your situation. You will need to know how much each item costs. Rarely should you discount the item below what you paid for it. You may offer certain products as "loss leaders" to attract customers; but if your prices are less than cost, you may be violating the law.

Your price discount will need to be enough to influence potential customers. If the item sells for $100, then a 5 percent discount probably will not change consumer behavior. You may need to offer a discount of at least 20 percent to attract customer interest. If the item is seasonal in nature and the season is over, then a larger discount may be needed for customers to justify buying it and storing it for six months before they can use it.

Some retailers do special discount promotions. They reduce the price by an additional 5 percent per day or week until the inventory is sold. This is known as a gambler's sale. The longer customers wait, the more they run the risk of the item being sold out before they can buy it.

You may also consider offering a quantity discount. Some businesses provide a discount if the customer buys a certain number of items. Tire retailers frequently run the sale, "Buy three tires and get the fourth free!" This comes out to a 25 percent discount on a set of four tires. Quantity discounts represent an avenue for reducing your inventory by encouraging your customers to buy more at one time.

Credit cards and charge accounts also have a bearing on price strategy. The primary reason for discounting is to make an item more affordable to potential customers. Some businesses have found that when customers charge purchases on their credit cards, they actually buy more items. The same applies to charge accounts. Furniture stores often let their customers charge items and postpone payments for six months or a year. They have learned that this strategy may attract more customer interest than a 10 percent–off sale. A note of caution may be appropriate here. Extending credit to your customers is a major decision. Be sure you think it through before offering it. You increase your recordkeeping expenses, need to have more money on hand to pay your bills, and run the risk that your customers may not pay their bills when you extend credit.

Odd-even pricing practices may also be worth considering. If your business is in a very price-competitive market, then you may consider using odd-number pricing. Retailers have found that when they offer a product at $9.97 instead of $10.00, it may increase sales. Research has shown that people frequently perceive a $9.97 item to be in the $9.00 category rather than in the $10.00 category even though it is only 3 cents from being a $10.00 item. The 3-cent difference may produce a psychological difference in some consumers' minds.

Odd-number pricing may not be appropriate for all businesses. K-mart may offer a man's shirt for $14.97, but Saks Fifth Avenue rarely has any item end with anything other than zeros. Its top-of-the-line clothes will be offered at prices in $45.00, $60.00, and $100.00 price lines which reflect different levels of quality. Saks wants to emphasize the quality of its products and their exclusiveness. Saks feels price competition is for businesses that offer products and services to people who have limited disposable income. Some prestigious businesses do not even list prices. They feel price is never an issue with certain target markets.

Pricing products and services is not a simple matter. Prices say something about your business and your target market. Consumers rely on prices to provide them with an indication of the quality of your products and services. The market will determine if your prices are too high, too low, or just right. If you do not offer the people in your target market what they want for the price you charge, they will consider your products and services to be expensive, possibly too expensive. If you give them more than they expected, then they will consider doing business with you to be a good deal. Your pricing strategy thereby plays a major role in whether you will be able to create and maintain customers for a profit.

6
Promotional Strategy and Physical Distribution Strategy

Once you have determined the products-services to offer and the most appropriate price range, you can shift your attention to developing your promotional strategy and your physical distribution strategy. Promotional strategy can be viewed as how you communicate with your target market. Physical distribution strategy refers to how businesses get their goods and services to their customers.

Promotional Strategy

There are various ways to communicate with potential customers. Promotional strategy includes advertising, publicity, sales promotions, personal selling, and public relations. Each component of the promotional mix plays a role in your effort to have potential customers learn about your business and buy your goods or services. Your promotional strategy must address the who, what, when, where, and how much money to spend.

The "Who" of Your Promotional Strategy

Your promotional strategy must use the rifle approach, discussed earlier. No business can be all things to all people, and no business has an unlimited amount of money to spend on its promotions. You will need to be sure you direct your effort and money to your target market.

The better you can identify who is in your target market, where they live, what magazines and newspapers they read, what television stations they watch, and what radio stations they listen to, the higher the probability that you will be able to get their attention and influence their behavior. This is why the customer profile is so important. If you can identify your target market's demographics, then you can check the listenership, viewership, and readership profiles for various media, including local radio stations, newspapers, magazines, and television stations. For example, if you are opening a clothing store and the primary target market is teenage girls, then you should review the Arbitron rating of radio listenership in your geographic area. Most radio stations have a copy of the ratings. You will be able to determine which radio station has the highest listenership in that age category. The A. C. Nielsen rating service does the same for television viewership.

The "What" of Your Promotional Strategy

The "what" involves determining the message you should communicate to your target market. Your promotional strategy is intended to take people who may have varying degrees of interest in your type of goods and services and get them to become your customers. This is why it is so important that you be able to identify your target market. When you open your business, your target market will comprise people who have never been your customers. You will need to know who they are, who they are currently buying from, why they are buying the goods and services, and to what extent they are still "customers in search of a business."

Your promotional strategy is intended to get the people in your target market to modify their behavior. The "message" you send to the people in your target market must be tailored to their mental frameworks. Your message must also provide the incentive for them to do business with you. Your promotional strategy should be based on: (1) Who do you want to influence? (2) What do you have to offer them that is better than the competition? and (3) What do I need to communicate to them to get them to become my customers?

Remember, a business venture will be successful only if it has a competitive advantage. If your target market does not know you exist and realize how you are better, then you will not succeed.

Your promotional strategy should emphasize your competitive advantage(s). Successful promotional strategies are based on the concept,

"If everyone is offering a steak, then you must sell your sizzle!" You must know what your target market values. Your strategy should highlight your business's "unique selling points." For example, if your target market is made up of elderly people who live in rural areas and your grocery store is the only one that offers a delivery service, then your promotional strategy should emphasize your competitive advantage.

Promotional strategy can be viewed as a step-by-step process. You want to get your target market's attention, to have them develop an interest in what you have to offer, and to have them check out your business.

The "who" and "what" must be synchronized. When you are about to open your business, your message should be "institutional" in nature. You want people to learn about your business, what it offers, where it is located, and when it is open. Your grand opening advertising is then followed with reminder advertising. You will need to stay in your target market's minds and keep them informed when you add new brands, offer new services, or have a special sale.

The "When" of Your Promotional Strategy

There are four major intervals for promoting your business. The first is preopening promotion. It is very important for a new business to generate customer interest before your business opens its doors. You want your target market to be anxious for your business to open.

Some businesses do "teaser" advertising. A teaser ad may be, "The countdown has begun; there are only 60 days until Johnson's Home Furnishings opens." This business may do teaser advertising by erecting a sign where the business will be located indicating, "Johnson's Home Furnishings—A new approach to retail merchandising will be located on this site!"

Toys 'R' Us announced in March that it would start construction of a new store in July and be open to the public in October. The announcement did not cost any money because the local newspaper ran a story about the popular store coming to town. The preopening promotion not only got every child's attention, it prompted children to save their money for the grand opening sale. The promotional strategy helped direct a large portion of the target market's attention and money away from Toys 'R' Us's competition.

Grand opening and preopening promotion are very important because you will need to generate as much sales as possible when you open your business. The sooner you sell your products and services, the greater your ability to meet your financial obligations and produce a positive cashflow.

Your business will also need to provide ongoing promotions. Your existing customers will need to be kept informed about developments in your business. You will also need to let potential customers learn about your business and its sizzle. Most new businesses tend to have a token grand opening promotion and do little after that. You need to develop an ongoing promotional program that will keep your business in your target market's minds. The old adage, "If you build a better mousetrap, the world will beat a path to your door," does not apply in today's marketplace. If the world doesn't know about your mousetrap's advantages and the market doesn't know where your door is, then you will not sell a single mousetrap.

There may also be occasions when you should have special promotions. If you plan to have a two-for-one sale or a midnight madness sale, or add a new product or service, then you need to have a special promotion to notify your target market.

Your promotional strategy must include a timetable that reflects when you plan to do various promotional events. Your schedule will help you identify when you will need to offset slow periods with special promotions. The schedule will also provide a basis for projecting the timing of promotion-related expenses.

The "Where" of Your Promotional Strategy

Your promotional strategy will only be effective if its message gets to your target audience at the appropriate time. The "where" of promotional strategy involves the media you use to communicate with your target market. There are numerous avenues or media available for promoting your business. The key is to know which media will produce the best results. The media to be used will depend on to whom you want to direct your message, the nature of the message, and when it needs to be presented.

Each type of media has advantages and disadvantages. Television offers color, movement, sound, and broad geographic coverage. Radio offers a means to get to a large number of people at various times of the day and night. Newspapers offer daily coverage to a large percentage of an area's households. Direct mail permits you to send your message to a specific group of people. Billboards take advantage of a captive audience while people are in their automobiles.

There is no one best medium for all businesses. There is no one best medium for every type of message. If you plan to open a retail sailboat outlet, then it may be worth your while to do television advertising. After all, you are not selling sailboats; you are offering excitement, freedom, and fun. Television can capture the sizzle of your product or service. You may want to do occasional newspaper ads that provide pictures of your products and feature special promotions. Also consider using direct mail to people who live in neighborhoods with homes valued above $100,000. These people may fit your customer profile and probably have enough disposable income to afford your brand of sailboat.

Other businesses may find radio, billboard, and newspaper advertising to be more beneficial. Restaurants air radio ads during the morning rush hour to encourage drivers to try their businessperson's lunch special that day. The locations of billboards on major thoroughfares may also promote the restaurant's steak and seafood menu. That restaurant also may include an ad in Friday's newspaper that includes a coupon for a 20 percent discount or a free dessert.

When asked which medium is the best, the answer can only be, "The one that does the best job of attracting customers per dollar cost." Your promotion budget also influences media selection. You want to get the best return per dollar invested in promotion. One medium may cost less than another, but you need to determine which one will do the most effective job of getting your message to your target market. Businesses frequently evaluate media in terms of the cost of reaching each 1000 potential customers. This process serves as a good basis for comparing the media and for choosing the right radio station, television channel, etc. The *Standard Rate and Data Guide* may be helpful. It provides market information and media costs.

The "How Much" to Spend Part of Your Promotional Strategy

The question of how much money to spend on promoting your business is very difficult to answer. Some businesses spend a certain percentage of projected sales on promotion-related activities. If, for example, you are trying to generate sales of $100,000 for the first year, then you may want to review trade data on your type of business to learn what percentage of sales you should spend on advertising. Bank of America reports that the average ad expenses for apparel stores is 2 to 3 percent of sales; for bookstores, 1.5 to 2.5 percent of sales; and for gift stores, 1.5 to 2.5 percent of sales.

These figures reflect annual budgets for existing businesses. Your first year's promotional budget will need to be a larger percentage of sales because your business will be unknown and you will be trying to divert customers from other businesses. The percentage-of-sales method may provide a general idea of how much to spend, but spending a certain percentage of sales on promotion does not guarantee that you will generate that level of sales.

The best way to determine your promotional budget is to identify what you want to accomplish. This is known as the "target" approach. If you want to have 400 people come into your store each week, then you need to determine what type and amount of promotion you will need to do to achieve that goal. You may find it will take 3 prime-time radio spots per day on two different radio stations; a two-column, 3-inch ad in the local newspaper on Mondays, Wednesdays, and Fridays; 2 billboards located on two major thoroughfares; and 1000 direct-mail promotions per month to achieve your goal. The target approach recognizes that you must reach a "critical mass" before your promotions will have an effect on the market.

The percentage-of-sales approach indicates what businesses spent. The target approach determines what you think it will take to achieve your sales goal. The target approach is particularly appropriate for a new venture.

There are two other approaches businesses may use to determine their promotional budgets. Some businesses simply try to match their competition. They monitor the number of radio spots aired and the amount of ad space in the newspaper. The businesses then match their major competitor's promotional program. This approach has two flaws. First, it assumes that your competitors are doing the right type and amount of advertising. Second, if you don't do a better job of promoting your business than your competition, why should your target market do business with you?

The other approach to developing a promotional budget is based on how much you can afford to spend. This may be the least effective approach. It assumes that you have allocated money to all of the other aspects of your business. Any money that is left is what you can spend on promoting your business. The problem is that few businesses will have enough money left over in their budgets to do a good job. You must recognize that you need to do promotions to generate sales. If you hope to have enough sales to leave you with enough money to do promotions, then you have things backwards. You have to put the horse before the cart. Your promotional strategy needs to be developed as an integral part of your marketing mix and receive its fair share of your overall budget.

Cooperative advertising is one of the reasons you need to think about your promotional strategy when you are developing your product-service strategy. Some manufacturers offer cooperative advertising allowances to businesses that carry and promote their brands. The availability of cooperative advertising may provide the basis for selecting one brand over another if they are fairly comparable in quality, price, and image.

Manufacturers that offer cooperative advertising reimburse retailers who promote their brands from 10 to 100 percent of the retailers' advertising expenses. If the manufacturer offers a 50 percent allowance, this means the retailer can do twice as much advertising or cut the advertising budget in half. Cooperative advertising has another benefit. Manufacturers frequently provide camera-ready artwork for promotions. This will make your ads appear more professional and will enhance your business's image.

It is interesting to note that most people are reluctant to spend much money promoting their business. This reluctance is quite natural. Money spent on promotions offers no assurance that it will bring in enough customers to justify the expense. One of the sayings about advertising is, "Only one-half of advertising works. The problem is that you don't know in advance which half it will be!"

If you view promotion as an expense, you will probably shortchange your promotional budget. However, if you view it as an investment that is necessary to generate the level of sales needed to produce your targeted level of profit, then you may be more willing to allocate the money it deserves.

Your Promotional Mix

Most of the discussion of promotional strategy has been focused on advertising. Promotion also includes the name you choose for your business, its sign, personal selling techniques, point-of-purchase displays, special sales promotions, public relations, and publicity.

Publicity may be particularly important for a new business. Publicity is defined as media coverage for which you don't pay. Many radio stations, newspapers, and television stations do features on new businesses when they open. If your business is the first of its kind in your area or if it has some special "sizzle," you may be able to get the media to do a special feature on it. You should make every effort to get in touch with the media before your business opens. Publicity can be equivalent to thousands of dollars of free advertising. Publicity is also valuable because potential customers tend to pay more attention to features than to advertisements.

A final point needs to be made about your promotional strategy. The most effective form of promotion has not been mentioned. Undoubtedly, the best advertising is having a large number of satisfied customers. When you give people what they are looking for at a price that is reasonable, and in a convenient manner, you are creating a group of ambassadors for your business. Satisfied customers can be viewed as free salespeople.

The more that you provide satisfaction, the more your customers will recommend your business to other people. The more word-of-mouth recommendations, the less advertising you will need to pay for. The less money you need to spend on advertising, the lower your expenses. If you have lower expenses, then you can lower your prices. This will give you a price advantage over competitors who do not offer the same level of satisfaction. As you can see, product-service strategy, price strategy, promotional strategy, and physical distribution need to go hand in hand.

Physical Distribution Strategy

Physical distribution represents the way businesses provide goods and services to their customers. In some businesses, particularly retail businesses, the customer comes to the business. Their locations may be important. Service businesses usually go to the customer. Housepainters, landscapers, pool cleaners, and parking lot stripers are examples of service businesses that go to their customers. The location of their businesses is not very important.

Hairstyling, dry cleaning, shoe repair, and bookkeeping businesses are service businesses that have customers who usually come to the business. Their locations may be one of the most important parts of their marketing mixes. Some businesses never come into direct contact with their customers. More businesses are being started that promote their products via catalogs, take phone orders, and ship via the mail or commercial delivery services.

There is also a trend for retail businesses to deliver their products to their customers. Domino's grew at a phenomenal rate because its founder, Thomas Monoghan, realized that physical distribution could be its competitive advantage. If Domino's could deliver a warm pizza within 30 minutes, at a reasonable price, then it would attract customers who were in search of a business but preferred not to leave their residences to get a pizza.

Physical distribution strategy needs to be an integral part of the marketing mix. Too often, people go out and lease the first vacant facility they find. The location of your business may be the least flexible part of your marketing mix. You may be able to add or delete products or brands on a monthly basis. You can change your radio or newspaper ads almost overnight. Most businesses cannot change their locations with the same ease and speed.

You will have to do your homework before you select a location for your business. The location decision is like going fishing—you should find out where the fish are and fish there. Numerous new businesses fail each year because they were convenient to their owners rather than close to their target markets.

Trading-Area Analysis

The first step in determining the optimal location for your business is to identify your target market and your trading area. To use the fishing analogy again, you want to identify the type of fish that are in search of bait. Then you need to determine where they can be found.

If you want to determine which city may offer the best opportunity for your type of business, then your trading-area analysis should include a review of demographic information for each metropolitan area. Trading-area analysis lets you compare one city with another. Census data, the *State and Metropolitan Area Data Book*, and the *Survey of Buying Power* profile the population for most cities with a population in excess of 50,000 people. The *County and City Data Book* includes information about cities with more than 25,000 people and townships with more than 2500 people. The *Editor and Publisher Guide* and the other references listed in Chapter 4 will also be helpful.

You will be concentrating your attention on the nature of the population, not just the number of people in that geographic area. In most cases, you will be interested in how many people fit your customer profile rather than the overall population. It is possible for a city with 70,000 people to have more potential than a city twice its size. Staying with the fishing example, larger lakes don't necessarily have the largest fish. You will need to learn as much as possible about each trading area before you can determine the best one for your business.

Trading-area analysis helps you determine the number of people who fit your customer profile in each geographic area under consideration—the number of large fish in each lake. When you construct a competitive matrix for each area under consideration, you will learn the extent to which customers are still in search of a business—which lakes have the hungriest large fish. This way you will be able to rank cities under consideration according to which ones offer the greatest opportunity for a new venture. The competitive matrix will also indicate where potential customers live, where the competition is located, and the extent to which you may be able to use physical distribution strategy to develop a competitive advantage.

Your trading area can be defined as the geographic area you plan to serve. It can be divided into three zones. Your primary zone should constitute at least 66 percent of your expected sales volume. You expect two-thirds of your sales to be via customers who are located in this zone. Your secondary zone represents 15 to 25 percent of your sales volume. These customers may be located beyond your primary zone. They do business with you less often. Your tertiary zone represents customers who will only occasionally do business with you. They represent anywhere from 5 to 20 percent of your sales volume. The secondary and tertiary zones warrant your attention because they can make the difference between profit and loss.

If you are a retail business, your primary zone may be customers within a 10-minute drive of your location. Your secondary zone may be the people who are more than a 10-minute drive but less than one hour away. Your tertiary zone may include people who live beyond the secondary zone who make a special trip to your business. The radius of the zone may be defined in either miles or minutes. In any event, the size of each zone will vary with the type of business, the location of your competition, and your target market.

If you plan to set up a specialty business, each zone may be larger because people are willing to drive farther for your product or service. If you are going to open a convenience business, then your primary zone may be less than a three-minute drive. If you plan to have an impulse business, its primary market may be the people who drive or walk by your business.

The same guidelines may apply for a service business that calls on its customers. In this case, your prices may vary with each zone according to the difference in driving time and the cost of providing service calls.

If you plan to start a catalog business for food-related items with phone orders, your trading area may be the whole country. If you plan to offer specialty winter clothing, then your trading area might be the upper midwest and the northeastern part of the United States. Your secondary market may be the Plains States, the midwest, and the mid-Atlantic region. Your tertiary zone may be foreign markets with cold climates.

Choosing the Right Location

The process of locating your business can be viewed as traveling through a set of concentric circles. You start by selecting your overall trading area. Next you try to identify the best general location or neighborhood. Then you try to find the optimal site. It is usually helpful to take out a map and color in your target market. You then indicate the exact location of your competition. If your business needs to be close to its customers, then look for areas where your target market is not served at all or well enough by your competitors. The unserved areas may represent opportunities for developing a competitive advantage by having a better location.

Study each of the more promising neighborhoods to determine which one may provide the best opportunity for your new venture. You will be looking at the overall traffic flow, the nature of zoning requirements, accessibility by your target market, and the nature of the other businesses in that area. Certain neighborhoods offer greater opportunities than others. Once you identify the best area to locate your business, you are then in a position to look for the best facility and site.

Numerous factors need to be considered when you select the specific location for your business. One of the first things you will need to do is determine the nature and size of the facility needed for your business. If you need a drive-in window, at least 20 parking spaces, high visibility from the street, large windows, a rear door with a loading dock, at least 2500 square feet, and room to expand if your business is successful, then you will be in a position to compare various sites within that area. You may ask a commercial realtor to help you find a location to lease that fits your needs. If no facility is available, then the commercial realtor may be able to find someone who owns a favorable site who may be willing to build and lease a facility that will meet your particular needs.

The nature of your business will influence the type of facility you need and how important the exact site may be to your success. If you are a business that has customers who come to you, then your location could be very important. Potential customers often judge the quality of a business by the quality of its facility and its location. If you offer quality products and want to attract well-to-do customers, then your facility and location should be consistent with the image you want to project. You will also be judged by the businesses that are located next to your business and by the surrounding neighborhood.

You should try to locate near businesses that are already serving your target market but who will not be competing against you. An example may be a gourmet food shop. It may locate next to a high-fashion clothing boutique, a dry cleaner, a bookstore that specializes in hardcover books, and a French restaurant. The other businesses will be spending their promotional budgets to attract people who may also be in your target market to come to their businesses. This could reduce your promotional budget and increase your profits.

Most shopping malls try to create "symbiotic relationships" between their tenants. By having stores that appeal to similar segments, businesses help each other. This is particularly true with shopping items.

Some of the tenants in malls are called "parasite" businesses. They live off other businesses' customers. Impulse businesses frequently locate next to certain other businesses. They do little advertising. Instead, their locations serve as their promotional strategy. As noted earlier, cookie stands, flower stands, and popcorn stands use a parasite physical distribution strategy. They will select large regional shopping malls that offer high levels of pedestrian traffic. Impulse businesses are willing to pay high rental rates per square foot for their small spaces because they know their location may be just as important as the sight, smell, and taste of their products.

When someone asks, "How important is location to a new business?" the answer is, "It depends on the unique nature of the business, its target market, and its competition." Physical distribution strategy must be an integral part of your marketing mix. If your physical distribution strategy is not consistent with your product strategy, price strategy, and promotional strategy, then your business may fail. Conversely, if it is properly researched and planned, it could be one of your business's competitive advantages.

Be Prepared to Change Your Marketing Mix

One of the facts of business life is that the marketplace is in a constant state of change. Your customers' interests may change, new competitors may enter the market, new shopping malls may be built, and manufacturers of the brands you offer may go out of business. Almost everything may change in a relatively short period of time.

You must constantly monitor the market to detect changes and trends while they are occurring rather than after it is too late to change your marketing mix. If you are in tune with the changes and are able to modify your marketing mix to meet the changes, then you may be able to transform the changes into lucrative business opportunities.

7
Determining Your Initial Capital Requirement

If the marketing part of your business plan indicates that an opportunity exists for creating and maintaining customers, then it is time to determine if you can make a profit. In the financial part of the business plan you "run the numbers." Financial analysis will make it possible to estimate the amount of money needed to start your business as well as the profit that will be generated at varying levels of sales.

The financial part of the business plan gives you a chance to look before you leap. A good financial plan is a necessity today. If poor management is the number one cause of new business failure, then insufficient capital ranks second. Good financial planning facilitates business growth and enables financial control. The lack of financial planning, when coupled with poor financial practices, can destroy a business, even if a good market opportunity exists.

Business success requires having the right amount of funds, the right allocation of funds, and the right timing of funds. Your business plan must address the financial requirements for starting and operating your business.

Determining Your Initial Capital Requirement

Most people either fail to prepare an estimate or underestimate the amount of money needed to start their business. As business specialist

Maury Delmon noted, "The belief that a few thousand dollars and very hard work will buy success has held very little validity since the 1930s." Most first-timers have only a very hazy notion of the amount of cash, stock, or credit required to keep a business going until it can carry itself.

There are numerous ways to estimate the amount of money needed to start a business. The worksheet included in the U.S. Small Business Administration's (SBA) Checklist for Going into Business provides a good basis for figuring your initial capital requirement. (See Figure 7-1.) The SBA worksheet acknowledges the need to start a business with enough money to get it through the first few months. This is important, because when most people start a business, they tend to overestimate sales and underestimate expenses.

In the start-up stage, cash disbursements to cover operations usually go out more quickly than cash is received via sales. If you don't have enough money to meet your obligations to your landlord, suppliers, bank, employees, and all the other people who are an integral part of your business, your business may fail just as grapes often die on the vine from the lack of sun or rain.

Numerous businesses with profit potential never make it, because they run out of money. The SBA worksheet encourages the person starting a business to have the cash needed to meet the numerous contingencies found in the first months of operation. By having enough money up front, you should be able to make ends meet until you are able to generate a sufficient level of sales to cover cash outlays. Some businesses are able to have sales cover cash outlays in a few months, while other businesses may take at least a year for cash receipts to exceed cash disbursements. The SBA worksheet provides a quick estimate of your initial capital requirement. If the amount indicated by the SBA worksheet is within your reach, then you should have a CPA provide a more accurate estimate.

Estimating First Year's Sales

The first step in using the SBA worksheet is to estimate your first year's level of sales. This estimate is important because it serves as a basis for projecting various expenses. Unfortunately, estimating sales for a new business is probably the most difficult thing to do in starting a new venture.

There are numerous ways to estimate your first year's sales level. A good place to begin is to review *Census of Retail Trade* data, which reports total sales for your type of product or service in the geographic area you are planning to serve. If the census data indicates that the level

Estimated Monthly Expenses Item	Your estimate of monthly expenses based on sales of $ _____ per year	Your estimate of how much cash you need to start your business (See column 3.)	What to put in column 2 (These figures are typical for one kind of business. You will have to decide how many months to allow for in your business.)
	Column 1	Column 2	Column 3
Salary of owner-manager	$	$	2 times column 1
All other salaries and wages			3 times column 1
Rent			3 times column 1
Advertising			3 times column 1
Delivery expense			3 times column 1
Supplies			3 times column 1
Telephone and telegraph			3 times column 1
Other utilities			3 times column 1
Insurance			Payment required by insurance company
Taxes, including Social Security			4 times column 1
Interest			3 times column 1
Maintenance			3 times column 1
Legal and other professional fees			3 times column 1
Miscellaneous			3 times column 1
Starting Costs You Have to Pay Only Once			Leave column 2 blank
Fixtures and equipment			
Decorating and remodeling			Talk it over with a contractor
Installation of fixtures and equipment			Talk to suppliers from who you buy these
Starting inventory			Suppliers will probably help you estimate this
Deposits with public utilities			Find out from utilities companies
Legal and other professional fees			Lawyer, accountant, and so on
Licenses and permits			Find out from city offices what you have to have
Advertising and promotion for opening			Estimate what you'll use
Accounts receivable			What you neeed to buy more stock until credit customers pay
Cash			For unexpected expenses or losses, special purchases, etc.
Other			Make a separate list and enter total
Total Estimated Cash You Need To Start		$	Add up all the numbers in column 2

Figure 7-1. U.S. Small Business Administration's initial capital requirement worksheet.

of sales for that product or service was $2,500,000, then your next step is to estimate what share of the market of $2,500,000 you can attract in the first year.

Census data provides total sales figures as well as the number of establishments in that market. By reviewing the existing businesses, you can get a better idea of what level of sales each business may be doing. If there are currently five businesses of approximately equal size in terms of facilities and inventory, then the average sales per business may be around $500,000. It would be unusual for all the businesses to be the same size. Nevertheless, this process will give you a starting point for estimating your level of sales.

The next step involves estimating total sales for the market for the coming year. The census data may be a bit dated, so you would need to forecast what you think total sales will be the first year you are going to start your business. The overall level of sales in the marketplace could go up or down for various reasons. If the number of people who are likely to buy your type of services is expected to increase or if the existing customers are expected to have an increase in their disposable income, enabling them to buy more goods and services, then you would need to use a number larger than the $2,500,000 reported by the census as your overall estimate of sales. By reviewing census data trends for the last three or four years, you may be able to plot the direction and size of change that serve as the basis for trends. Economic and trade data may also be helpful here. You may learn that each household tends to spend $200 per year on your type of product or service. If your area is expected to have an increase of 800 households in the coming year, then sales should increase by at least $160,000.

If trade data reveals that for every increase of disposable income of $1000 per household, sales of your type of product increases by $20, then estimating the increase in disposable income will also serve as a basis for estimating how much overall sales will increase. Obviously, if the number of households and disposable income are expected to increase, overall sales could be quite a bit higher than the $2,500,000 reported in the census data. A note of caution should be taken here if your field of business is susceptible to inflationary pressures. Your economic-trend analysis of the past few years may project a 5 percent increase in sales per year. If inflation has been at the 5 percent level, the market may not actually be growing at all. Check to see if the number of units being sold is actually increasing. This may be a better indication of a growing market.

The child-care business may serve as a good example. Census data provides statistics on the number of households in a particular geographic area as well as the number of households with both parents (or a single parent) employed who have preschool-age children. These people could be primary customers of child-care services. The National Association for Child Care Management may provide an estimate of the expected annual rate of growth in the day-care industry. If the business census data does not indicate the overall level of money spent on day-care services in your area, then you could review the listing of day-care centers in the yellow pages. You could then call and ask how many children they have in each day-care facility as well as what is the weekly rate for child care. Basic math will give you a rough estimate of the total amount of money being spent on child care as well as the average level of sales for child-care businesses in your area.

This approach may not be very scientific, but in the absence of any other data, it will give you an idea about the level of business in the area. You could then look at the expected increase in the number of households, disposable income, and the rate of inflation to estimate what the overall level of sales may be for the coming year.

Estimating Target Market Potential

Once you have estimated the overall level of sales for your geographic area, you need to estimate sales for the segment of the overall market you believe will offer you the greatest opportunity. Your target market may be one geographic part of the overall market, one particular age group within the overall market, or a combination of these and other factors.

If your estimate of total sales for the overall geographic area for the year you plan to open your business is $2,700,000, then you need to determine what percent of the overall market your target market represents. If your target market comprises customers who live in certain neighborhoods, have a certain level of income, and are within a certain age range, then you could review census data to determine what percentage your target market represents of the overall market. Trade data may also provide statistics on what portion of overall sales is made by each segment of the market. Trade data may reveal that 70 percent of all purchases are made by people between the ages of 30 and 50 who have incomes greater than $40,000 and who live in homes valued at more than $120,000. You would then be in a position to estimate the portion that your target market represents of the overall market. If your analysis of trade and census data reveals that your target market represents 40 percent of overall spending ($2,700,000) on that type of product or service, then you would project your target market's sales to be $1,080,000.

Estimating Your Market Share

Now you have to estimate what percentage of your target market's sales you expect to capture from existing competition and obtain from new consumers or households entering your area. Your market share will be affected by the number, size, and effectiveness of the businesses already competing for the customers in your target market. Given your planned location, the size of its facilities, and the other parts of your marketing mix, you believe you can get 10 percent of the target market. This means you expect to attract some of the people who are moving into your area, some of the customers of the existing businesses who are still "in search of a business," as well as the people who have foregone buying because no business has offered them what they are looking for. In this case, a 10 percent share of this segment of your target market would be sales of $108,000.

Remember, this is a rough estimate. There is no guarantee that you will have sales of $108,000. This estimate is based on numerous assumptions, not the least of which is your ability to make the right decisions about your location, facility, types of services, level of inventory, price strategy, and the amount and type of advertising.

There are a couple of other ways to get an idea of your first year's sales. If you are going to start a retail business selling products, then you should ask the people who are going to be your suppliers what they think you can generate in the first year. Suppliers may be calling on and selling to the businesses in your territory. Suppliers may be in a good position to estimate the "average" level of sales for the other businesses. One note of caution, however: While the suppliers want to help you, they also want you to buy what they are selling. Some suppliers may overestimate what you can do just to get you to buy more inventory in the beginning. After all, they may be on commission and they wouldn't want you to run the risk of being out of inventory if you are successful in attracting customers.

Another approach to get a feel for possible levels of sales is to see if your type of business is listed in publications like *Robert Morris Associates, Inc.'s Annual Statement Studies, The Almanac of Business and Financial Ratios* (Prentice-Hall), and the *Accounting Corporation of America's Barometer of Small Business*, which provide financial information about numerous businesses. Some of these publications categorize firms by total asset size or level of sales. Even though the businesses that report their financial statistics to these publications may not be a perfectly representative sample of all businesses of that type, they do provide an idea of the percentage of businesses that have assets or sales less than $100,000, $500,000, $1,000,000, etc.

The financial tables may indicate that 90 percent of all businesses have sales less than $250,000. If so, it would be unlikely for your business to exceed that level of sales unless your market was much larger, your competition much weaker, and your business significantly bigger and better than almost all businesses of that type. The same logic also applies to the amount of assets required to support certain levels of sales. Financial analysis reveals a direct correlation between sales and assets. In other words, it takes a certain level of assets (facilities, inventory, fixtures, etc.) to support a certain level of sales.

The sales-to-assets ratio is an important one to keep in mind because it indicates that for certain businesses, for every $10,000 in sales, an additional $5000 in assets is needed of which $2000 will be for inventory, $500 for additional fixtures, $2000 for additional space, and $500 for receivables and cash. As you can see, if you can estimate your first year's sales, you should be in a position to start estimating your initial capital requirement.

Identifying Your Cash Outlays

Now that you have an estimate of your first year's sales, you are in a position to complete the rest of the SBA worksheet. As noted earlier, a business needs to have a certain level of assets to support a specific level of sales. The SBA worksheet lists most of the types of assets and cash outlays you will have to address when starting a business.

The SBA worksheet asks you to identify and list all the aspects of your business that will require cash outlays. The worksheet divides cash outlays into two categories: those that are regular cash outlays and those that are one-time cash outlays associated with opening your business.

Estimating Monthly
Cash Outlays

First, you need to identify and list all the recurring monthly cash outlays. Next, you need to estimate the cash needed for each outlay and record this amount in column 1. Column 2 reflects the cash required to make it through the first few months when your business is getting off the ground.

The SBA worksheet encourages the prospective owner to have at least three months' working capital available. You might say, "Surely I will sell something during the first 90 days, so I shouldn't need to start with 90 days of money without sales." A better way to look at the 90-day equivalent is to view it as having enough money to cover your first six months of operations if sales are only one-half what you expect.

The 90-day equivalent increases your chances of beating the odds, because it gives you a buffer against lower-than-expected sales and higher-than-expected outlays. Remember, the number-two reason for business failure is insufficient funds. Don't get caught making the mistake too many first-timers make. It is safe to say, "If you don't have enough money from the start, you won't be able to obtain it when you run out." Good financial management begins with (1) carefully estimating the amount of money needed, (2) knowing how much will be needed during your first year until revenue from sales can cover your cash outlays, and (3) having good financial controls to insure that you are using your money the best way.

Owner's or Manager's Salary

If you plan to manage your business, you should fill in the amount you plan to withdraw to pay yourself. The SBA worksheet guidelines recommend that you double the figure in column 1 and place this figure in column 2. The rationale for a multiple of 2 is that if your business is running short on cash, you may be able to forego some or all of your salary until things get better. If you plan to hire someone to manage the business, then you should put three times the manager's salary in column 2. The manager may be less willing to postpone his or her paycheck.

If you plan to hire a manager, remember: you get what you pay for. Be sure you hire someone who has already demonstrated the ability to run a successful business. The best way to avoid the number-one reason for business failure—poor management—is to be willing to pay for quality management. Don't cut corners here. The quality of the manager's decisions will determine your business's chances for success more than anything else.

Salaries and Wages

This amount can be estimated by multiplying: (1) the number of people other than the manager who will be employed, (2) the hours they will work, and (3) their hourly wage rates. If you are planning to start a service business, your people will be your "products." Your estimate of salaries and wages is particularly important if you plan a service business, because this may be your largest cash outlay per month.

You may be tempted to pay your employees the minimum wage. Again, you tend to get what you pay for. If you plan to be better than your competitors, you should recognize that the quality of your employees will affect your chances for success. If you are trying to create and maintain customers, you must recognize that employee relations and customer relations are closely interrelated. As someone once said, "If all you offer is peanuts, then you should not be surprised when you end up with a bunch of monkeys!" If you cut corners with your people, they will cut corners with you and your customers.

Rent

Various factors need to be considered when estimating rent. The first question to be answered is how much space you need. Trade association data can be helpful here. Most associations compute average annual sales per square foot. If the trade association for your type of business indicates $100 sales per square foot, then you would need a 1100-square-foot facility for your business if you are trying to generate $108,000 annual sales.

You may need more space if you plan to carry more inventory or have more open space than the average business. If you expect your business to grow substantially in the second year, you may need to lease more than a 1100-square-foot facility so that you won't be forced to seek a new facility if things go well.

The next step is to find a facility that is convenient to your target market. The facility will also need to provide the right image, atmosphere, and surrounding businesses for your business to be able to attract potential customers. Remember, your decision about a location and a facility must be closely tied to your target market and your desire to create a competitive advantage.

Annual retail rent rates may range from $2 to $100 per square foot, depending on the city, size of facility, and ancillary services. If an appropriate facility rents for $8 per square foot, then you need to divide the annual rent of $8800 by 12 to figure your monthly cash outlay for rent. Multiply the $734 monthly rate by 3 and put the $2202 in column 2. Some lease rates are based on a percentage of sales when your sales go beyond a certain level. If you expect your level of sales to exceed the specified level, use the monthly percentage as the basis rather than the square-foot figure. In this example, sales would not be expected to exceed the standard ($8500 per month, or $100,000 per year) until late in the year, so the square-foot figure is used.

You may be tempted to save money by leasing a vacant facility which is available on a monthly lease that is markedly lower than other locations. Be careful: Most facilities are vacant because the last business located there went bankrupt. This is not a good omen. Also, any money saved by getting an out-of-the-way location will have to be made up with more advertising, lower prices, etc. A good thing to remember is "Out of sight…out of mind!" You don't attract customers by having them play hide and seek with your business.

Advertising

There are various ways to estimate the amount you need to spend on advertising. One method relies on trade data. Trade data may indicate that businesses offering your types of goods and services spend a certain percentage of sales on advertising. The percentage varies from one type of business to another. It may also be a higher or lower percentage based on the size of the business. In any event, trade data will give you an idea about what similar businesses, possibly your competitors, may be spending on advertising.

Another approach to determining how much to spend on advertising is to estimate the amount and type of advertising it will take to achieve the desired ($108,000) level of sales. As a new business, you will have to "create" your customers. Advertising will play a significant role in this process.

By knowing your target market, you should be able to determine the number of television, radio, newspaper, direct-mail, and other type of ads you will need to use to get the attention and interest of your prospective customers. Your advertising will also need to attract potential customers, get them to try your business as soon as possible, and stay on customers' minds after they have tried you.

Your estimate also needs to take into consideration the nature, level, timing, and effectiveness of your competition's advertising. If a significant portion of your first year's sales is to come from winning customers from your competition, then your advertising budget will have to be larger than your competitors' advertising budgets.

Advertising is not a science, and there are no guarantees. One thing is certain: If you cut corners on your advertising, you will probably be cutting your throat. If your sales goal is $108,000 and trade data indicates that 3 percent of sales is spent on advertising, spending $3240 per year, or $270 a month, will not assure you of $108,000 in sales. Your message, media, timing, marketing mix, and competition, among other things, will affect your level of sales as much as your advertising budget.

Delivery Expenses

Trade association data can be helpful here. Delivery expenses tend to be proportional to sales. Trade data may indicate that ½ percent of sales is spent on delivery expenses. Another way to estimate delivery expenses is to figure what you will need to have delivered for the first three months. This figure would be placed in column 2. Trade data may be useful for estimating annual delivery expenses, but this approach may be better for the SBA worksheet. If you plan to ship or deliver your products to your customers, then delivery costs will need to be included in the worksheet.

Supplies

This estimate can be handled the same way as delivery expenses. You can use trade data or list all the supplies you will need on a monthly basis for the first three months.

Telephone

The best way to get an estimate of telephone expenses would be to identify all the long-distance calls you are planning to make. Most of your calls will be to suppliers. Costs for these calls can then be added to your regular monthly phone bill. The charge for your yellow page ad should be listed in the advertising account instead of in the telephone entry. For many businesses, this may not be a major outlay. However, some businesses rely extensively on the phone. In any event, the larger the amount that may be spent on any expense, the greater the need for an accurate estimate of the monthly amount.

Other Utilities

Your utility expenses will vary with the type and size of your facility. If you are going to be renting a facility that is at least a few years old, the leasing agent or prior tenant may be able to tell you what the utility expenses were in the past. If you are planning to lease new space or build a new facility, the utility companies serving that area should be willing to provide an estimate of the utility expenses for your size and type of facility for little or no charge.

Insurance

Trade data may be helpful here, but this estimate can be provided by a commercial insurance broker or agent. Ask three different commercial insurers to review your proposed business, present a "Business Owner's Package," all risk insurance coverage proposal, and tell you the price for coverage. This should be at no charge to you. The rate is usually based on the nature of your business, the type of structure it is located in, and the total value of the assets to be covered. If your business is quite different from most businesses, seek a broker who has an underwriter on the staff. The underwriter may be able to prepare a package that reflects the uniqueness of your business. This will be better and, in some cases, less expensive than a standard package. Insurance is like advertising. Most people would rather not spend money for it. But it is far better to be safe by having too much than to be sorry for spending too little. Too many profitable businesses have gone bankrupt because their owners tried to save a few dollars by not having sufficient insurance coverage.

Taxes and Payroll-Related Outlays

Most businesses will have to pay for a sales-use tax license if they will be selling products or services at the retail level. This is usually an annual charge. The sales tax you charge will not be recorded here because customers pay that tax. This section of the SBA worksheet includes all payroll-related taxes and charges incurred by the employer. The major outlays are social security, unemployment, and workers' compensation coverage. Social security (also known as FICA) is paid by both the employer and employee. The rate for social security is a specific percentage of payroll up to a certain amount of annual income per employee. The rate usually goes up every other year. The ceiling usually goes up in alternating years. If your business is formed as a proprietorship and you will be working in the business, you will be required to pay a self-employment tax as part of social security. The rate tends to be just less than twice the individual rate up to the same income ceiling that you take out of the business, because you are both the employer and employee. The rate and ceiling for the self-employment tax change as often as the individual social security rate and ceiling.

Employers are expected to pay a federal unemployment tax. The rate is a percentage of each employee's wages up to a certain level of income. Many states also have an unemployment tax. If a state has an unemployment tax, then the percentage of tax is deducted from the percentage of the federal tax to determine what is owed for the federal tax. Some states do not limit their tax to the same ceiling used by the federal government. Most employers are also expected to pay for workers' compensation coverage for their employees. The rate will depend on the nature of the business and the number of employees. The rate may range from less than 1 percent to over 6 percent of payroll. Property taxes and privilege licenses should also be included in your estimate.

Interest

Your monthly cash outlay for interest can be determined only after you have made the first estimate of your initial capital requirement. If the amount of cash you need to start your business is larger than the amount you have of your own money, in combination with a partner, or via the issuance of corporate stock, you will probably need to borrow money. Whether you borrow from a bank, a Small Business Investment Corporation (SBIC), or some other lender, you will have interest payments.

If the first estimate of your initial capital requirement indicates that you will need to borrow $20,000, then you will have to revise your estimate to include interest (and possibly principal) payments in columns 1 and 2. This row on the SBA worksheet should be renamed "loan payments" to more accurately reflect the money you will need to repay the loan on a monthly basis.

You may be able to secure a five-year loan for $20,000 with only interest due on a monthly basis. You would then be expected to make a "balloon" payment of $20,000 on the principal of the loan at the end of five years. You may, however, be expected to have your loan "amortized" like a short-term mortgage, with equal monthly payments over the five years covering principal and interest. With amortization, there would be no balloon payment due at the end of the loan. For example, if you borrow $20,000 at 11 percent with monthly payments for interest and a balloon payment of the $20,000 due at the end of the loan, your monthly interest payment of $184 would appear in column 1. If you were required to amortize your loan, you would put $435 in column 1. Obviously, the interest-only monthly payment with a balloon payment due at the end of the loan will reduce your initial capital requirement. You may even secure a loan with a 15-year amortization schedule with a 5-year balloon payment for all the outstanding principal. However, you will need to establish a "sinking fund" from each year's profits to cover the balloon payment when it comes due. The amortized loan reduces the need for self-discipline because it is structured like a sinking fund.

Once you have recorded the appropriate figure in column 1, recompute the total initial capital requirement. This will increase the amount you need to borrow and the amount of your monthly payments. As you can see, you are not in a position to put a number in the interest row until you have figured all the other cash outlays and your loan obligation.

Maintenance Expenses

Maintenance outlays will be related to the type and size of your facility. If you are leasing space, your lease agreement may specify a certain amount of required maintenance for your space and common areas like parking places, restrooms, etc. If not, you will need to estimate your monthly cash outlays by contacting potential maintenance services.

Legal and Other Professional Fees

Again, trade data may be helpful in estimating outlay for legal and professional services. However, it may be better to get estimates from a few attorneys and accountants. Accounting fees usually constitute a major professional expense. The monthly outlay for accounting services will be affected by the nature and size of your business. Your fees will also be influenced by whether you or the accountant prepare month-end and quarterly statements. The fees will also vary if you hire a bookkeeping service, an accountant, or a CPA. Each level and type of service has a different price tag.

You should ask the people you know who already are in business for people they would recommend. You can then ask a couple of the recommended accounting services to review your type of operation and give you an estimate of their fee structure for various levels of service.

Legal expenses represent the other major type of professional fee. Business operations usually involve contracts. You may also find it necessary to seek legal advice on a regular basis. The same approach to selecting an accountant should be used when selecting an attorney. In any event, select an attorney who specializes in commercial law. The estimate for professional fees is important. This outlay could range from about a hundred dollars to over a thousand dollars per month.

Miscellaneous Expenses

In running a business, there are always a few things that come up each month that require funds. You may make a contribution to a local charity or buy flowers for an employee who is ill. These cash outlays may be labeled "miscellaneous" because you don't know when they will occur from month to month. However, there is always something that adds to your cash outlay. Accordingly, you need to plan ahead and budget for miscellaneous outlays.

Starting Costs You Only Have to Pay Once

All your estimates so far have involved recurring cash outlays. The time has come to estimate outlays that are associated with starting a business. The estimate for each outlay will be recorded in column 2.

Fixtures and Equipment

You need to determine what fixtures you will need to furnish your business. You should talk to suppliers and contractors to get estimates for counters, storage shelves, cabinets or display stands, a cash register, special lighting, an outside sign, etc. At this point, you should decide whether you will be buying these items or leasing them. If you buy the fixtures, you will make a one-time outlay. If you lease them, you will have monthly payments. You should treat your lease as a monthly outlay by recording three times your monthly lease rate in column 2 or by placing it in the upper half of your worksheet. Obviously, leasing your equipment will reduce your initial capital requirement. Leasing also provides flexibility. By leasing equipment, it should be possible to upgrade or change your equipment to meet your needs as your business grows and changes. In any event, be sure that your attempt to reduce your initial capital requirement does not jeopardize your chances for being profitable. Take a close look at the lease terms as well as the penalties associated with the lease.

Decorating and Remodeling

Almost every facility requires remodeling. Ask two or three contractors for written bids before selecting one.

Installation of Fixtures and Equipment

This outlay is treated separately from the acquisition of fixtures and equipment because first-timers often forget to figure the cost of having these items installed. Also, if you did not include the cost of having these items shipped or delivered in the purchase or lease figure, it should be reported here. This illustrates one of the benefits of compiling a list of cash outlays. You reduce the likelihood of leaving something out and having too little cash to meet your obligations.

Starting Inventory

This can be the most significant cash outlay for a new business. If you plan to start a retail business, your inventory could represent at least half of your initial capital requirement. If you plan to start a service business, you may not have much inventory because your people really serve as your inventory.

The best way to estimate your inventory needs will be to figure how much will need to be on hand to support the level of sales you projected earlier for the first year of your business. There is a simple set of calculations you can follow to get an estimate of your initial inventory if you have access to trade data. You need to find out what is the average percentage markup on cost. You also need to find out what is the "stock turn." The stock-turn ratio indicates how many times your average inventory turns, or is sold, during the year. For example, merchandise in an antiques shop may turn two times a year. This means that the average item takes about six months to be sold. Merchandise in a clothing store may turn six times. This means that the average shirt is in inventory for two months before being sold. The stock-turn ratio is computed by dividing your projected first year's cost of goods sold by the expected average inventory.

$$\text{Stock-turn ratio} = \frac{\text{annual cost of goods sold}}{\text{average inventory}}$$

Trade data usually provides a breakdown of income statement and balance sheet information. Trade data may indicate that the cost of goods sold is 50 percent of sales. If this is what you expect for your business, then you expect that items will be sold for twice the price you paid for them. If the stock-turn ratio for your type of business is 3, then you can use the following two-step process to estimate the amount of inventory you will need to start your business:

Step 1

Multiply the projected level of sales $108,000
by the percentage that cost of goods
   sold is of sales (50%)   ×   .50
to get your estimated cost of goods sold $ 54,000

Step 2

Divide your cost of goods sold $\frac{\$54,000}{3} = \$18,000$
by the stock-turn ratio

You will need $18,000 in inventory to support sales of $108,000. A note of caution needs to be made here. This is an estimate. Starting your business with $18,000 in inventory will not guarantee $108,000 in sales, just as having a certain number of square feet or spending a certain amount on advertising will not guarantee $108,000 in sales. The brands you offer, the way you display your merchandise, the effectiveness of your advertising, the appeal of your location, etc., will influence your level of sales. Also, you may have fewer stock turns because you are a new business. Charging higher prices usually reduces your stock turn.

You also need to consider whether your business is seasonal in nature. If you are starting in a peak season, you will need more inventory. You will need to carry a larger inventory if it will take considerable time to replenish it or if the cost of a stock out (lost business by not having an item in stock when a customer wants it) is high. Suppliers may help you to estimate your inventory needs. They are familiar with the needs of similar-sized businesses.

Deposits With Public Utilities

Most utility (phone, electricity, sewer, water, etc.) companies require a deposit from new businesses. Contact each utility to learn deposit requirements.

Legal and Other Professional Fees

Even though you listed professional fees in the estimated monthly outlays part of the worksheet, you still need to record the costs incurred in establishing the legal form for your business and setting up the accounting records. These are one-time expenses that need to be treated separately from your ongoing cash outlays. These expenses will vary in proportion to the size, nature, and complexity of your new business.

If you plan to start your business as a corporation, the cost may run from a few hundred to a few thousand dollars to prepare the articles of incorporation, set up the bylaws, and get the corporate record books and seal in order. The same is true for having an accountant set up your books.

Licenses and Permits

License and permit requirements vary with each type of business. You should check with state, county, and city offices to learn what is required for your business. Certain businesses need a "privilege" license. You may also need to secure a retail or wholesale sales license. There also may be charges for construction permits or inspections.

Advertising and Promotions for Grand Opening

Your grand opening advertising covers all the advertising that precedes and coincides with the opening of your business. This amount is separate from your regular monthly advertising budget. You will need to determine the level of visibility you want for your business. This is an important initial expense, because you want people to start buying your goods or services as soon as your business opens. Remember, the longer it takes to create customers, the more money you will need for your initial capital.

Suppliers and media representatives can be helpful here. One rule of thumb for estimating grand opening advertising is that you should spend at least three times the amount you allocated for one month's regular advertising.

Accounts Receivable

Now may be a good time to bring up a caution about accounts receivable. There is one good type of accounts receivable—the one with a zero balance. This is one of the most frustrating aspects of running a business. If at all possible, have your customers charge their purchases on their bank credit cards. Credit cards may cost a small percentage of sales revenue, but monitoring them will take far less time than keeping track of the credit that you extend to customers. You will also reduce the likelihood of having bad-debt losses.

If you plan to let your customers charge their purchases "on account" to you, then you will need to have more money to start your business. You need to estimate the average balance for your accounts receivable. If you expect to have $2500 in accounts receivable, then you will need to include this figure in the initial capital requirement estimate.

Cash

Most businesses need to have cash on hand or readily available to meet unexpected cash obligations and to handle daily operations. Contact the owners or managers of similar businesses in other cities. They should be

Estimated Monthly Expenses Item	Your estimate of monthly expenses based on sales of $ 108,000 per year	Your estimate of how much cash you need to start your business (See column 3.)	What to put in column 2 (These figures are typical for one kind of business. You will have to decide how many months to allow for in your business.)
	Column 1	Column 2	Column 3
Salary of owner-manager	$ 1,500	$ 3,000	2 times column 1
All other salaries and wages	700	2,100	3 times column 1
Rent	750	2,202	3 times column 1
Advertising	405	1,215	3 times column 1
Delivery expense	45	135	3 times column 1
Supplies	22	66	3 times column 1
Telephone and telegraph	50	150	3 times column 1
Other utilities	67	200	3 times column 1
Insurance	42	126	Payment required by insurance company
Taxes, including Social Security	292	1,168	4 times column 1
Interest	435	1,305	3 times column 1
Maintenance	20	60	3 times column 1
Legal and other professional fees	100	300	3 times column 1
Miscellaneous	40	120	3 times column 1
Starting Costs You Have to Pay Only Once			Leave column 2 blank
Fixtures and equipment		4,000	
Decorating and remodeling		3,000	Talk it over with a contractor
Installation of fixtures and equipment		200	Talk to suppliers from who you buy these
Starting inventory		18,000	Suppliers will probably help you estimate this
Deposits with public utilities		150	Find out from utilities companies
Legal and other professional fees		350	Lawyer, accountant, and so on
Licenses and permits		100	Find out from city offices what you have to have
Advertising and promotion for opening		1,215	Estimate what you'll use
Accounts receivable		0	What you need to buy more stock until credit customers pay
Cash		1,000	For unexpected expenses or losses, special purchases, etc.
Other		200	Make a separate list and enter total
Total Estimated Cash You Need To Start		$ 40,362	Add up all the numbers in column 2

Figure 7-2. Completed initial capital requirement worksheet.

willing to give you an idea of the amount of cash they have on hand to meet their needs.

Other

It is hoped that your estimates include all of your money needs. It may be helpful to play it safe by having an extra few hundred dollars on the sidelines.

Completing the
SBA Worksheet

You can now estimate your initial capital requirement. Add the one-time cash outlays to the total for column 2 of the monthly cash outlays. The total represents a rough estimate of the amount of money you need up-front to open your business and keep it open until your customers provide enough money to cover expenses and make a profit. (See Figure 7-2.)

8
Projecting the Financial Status for the First Years

Now that you have figured your initial capital requirement you are in a position to determine if you have enough money to start your business. If you don't have enough money, you will have to decide whether you want to: (1) seek additional funding via a partner or loans, or by forming a corporation and selling stock, (2) scale down your business to fit the money you have, (3) postpone starting your business until you have enough money, (4) consider one of the other possible businesses you identified earlier, or (5) drop the idea of starting your own business altogether.

If you have enough money to start your business, then you are ready to go to the next step of your financial plan—preparing financial projections for the first three to five years of operation. Several important questions need to be answered. The first question is, "What kind of profit can be expected for the first year?"

You went through a fairly deliberate process to estimate your first year's sales when figuring your initial capital requirement. Now you need to be sure that your first year's sales estimate will generate a sufficient level of profit to yield a good return on the money you will invest in the business and to provide enough money to expand your operations. If you need to borrow money to start your business, the level of profit you expect to make will be very important to potential lenders. Sales may pay interest, but profits will be needed to pay off the principal of the loan.

Profit Planning: Conducting Cost-Volume-Profit Analysis

The first step of your financial analysis is to estimate the expected profit for your first year at your projected level of sales. The second step involves figuring the resulting profit or loss at various sales levels for your first year. This is called cost-volume-profit analysis.

In the example used earlier, you estimated $108,000 for your first year's sales. You need to identify all your expenses and determine how much each expense will be for the first year. Cost of goods sold may represent your largest single expense. In this example, if you buy the items for $5 and sell them for $10, then your cost of goods sold will be one-half of sales. This is the same as a markup of 100 percent on cost or 50 percent of sales.

If you expect to sell $108,000 during the first year, then your cost of goods sold will be $54,000. This tells you that you will have $54,000 left from sales to cover your other expenses and hopefully provide you with enough profit to justify your time, risk, and financial investment. Next, you estimate all the other expenses for your business. Most, if not all, of these expenses will be relatively fixed, such as rent, advertising, payroll, insurance, etc. Add the selling and administrative expenses (including depreciation expenses) for the year to your cost of goods sold to determine your total expenses. When you deduct total expenses, including your start-up expenses of $4865 (for decorating, installation, legal fees, licenses, and grand opening advertising; the other one-time outlays are not considered expenses), from the $108,000 sales figure, you will get your pretax profit or loss for your first year.

Sales	$ 108,000	100%
Cost of goods sold	−54,000	−50
Gross margin	$ 54,000	50%
Selling, administrative, and interest expenses	−57,528	−53
Profit or (loss) before taxes	$ (3,528)	− 3%

At this time, you should check your projections with financial data, such as *Robert Morris Associates, Inc.'s Annual Statement Studies*. As noted earlier, trade data provides ratios for cost of goods sold, gross margin, selling and administrative expenses, profit as a percentage of sales, and numerous other important statistics that will help you estimate certain figures. This process is also helpful to verify whether your estimates are in line with other similar businesses.

Estimating the first year's profit or loss is an essential part of your financial plan. If you find that the first year's sales will not yield a profit, this is not very encouraging. Keep in mind, however, that few businesses, even those that become financially successful, generate a profit in their first year.

If you project a loss, you need to determine if it is too large for you to handle. If your projections for the second year include a significant increase in sales and a large enough profit to make up for the loss you incurred in the first year while "learning the ropes" and establishing your business, then you may still consider going ahead with starting your business. If your projections are not any better for the second, third, and fourth years, you should take a good hard look at whether this is the right business to start.

Cost-volume-profit analysis is a particularly helpful approach for evaluating a potential business venture. If you can estimate your cost of goods sold, which will vary with the level of sales, as well as the other expenses that are relatively stable or fixed, then you can estimate the profit or loss for your business at various levels of sales. You can also calculate the level of sales it will take to break even—where your revenue covers your expenses.

The following example illustrates how cost-volume-profit analysis can give you an idea of how to make various estimates:

1. If your cost of goods sold is expected to be 50 percent of sales, then your gross margin will be 50 percent of sales.

2. Divide the fixed expenses by the gross margin percentage of sales.

3. If your fixed expenses are expected to be $50,000, then you have the following equation:

$$\frac{\text{Fixed expenses}}{\text{Gross margin as a percentage of sales}} = \text{breakeven in sales}$$

$$\frac{\$50,000}{.50} = \$100,000$$

This formula indicates that your breakeven point in sales is $100,000. The breakeven level of sales is reflected in the following simplified income statement:

Sales	$ 100,000	100%
Cost of goods sold	−50,000	−50
Gross margin	$ 50,000	50%
Selling and administrative expenses	−50,000	−50
Profit before taxes	$ 0	0%

Your business will not begin making a profit unless sales exceed $100,000. Your breakeven point is important, because for every dollar of sales beyond your breakeven of $100,000, you get a 50-cent profit. If your sales forecast falls below your breakeven point, then you will need to have additional money on the sidelines to put into your business to keep it afloat until sales exceed expenses.

Cost-volume-profit analysis has another benefit. It permits you to calculate the level of sales needed to generate a certain level of profit. If you want to know the level of sales needed to produce a $10,000 profit, then you add the desired level of profit to the fixed expenses and do the same computation:

$$\frac{\text{Fixed expenses plus profit goal}}{\text{Gross margin as a percentage of sales}} = \begin{array}{l}\text{Sales to generate a}\\ \text{certain level of profit}\end{array}$$

$$\frac{\$50,000 + \$10,000}{.50} = \$120,000$$

The estimate can be reflected in the following income statement:

Sales	$ 120,000	100.0%
Cost of goods sold	−60,000	−50.0
Gross margin	$ 60,000	50.0%
Selling and administrative expenses	−50,000	−41.7
Profit before taxes	$ 10,000	8.3%

It is important to note the effect that varying levels of markup or fixed costs may have on your breakeven point and the corresponding profit and loss estimates for various levels of sales. The following examples may illustrate the point:

Example 1: Varying Your Markup

Let's say you enter a market where price competition is intense or you choose to offer lower prices than your competition. You decide to have your markup on cost be 66.7 percent. This is the same as a markup on sales of 40 percent. Your cost of goods sold will then be 60 percent of sales. If you paid $5 for an item, your selling price will be $8.33 instead of the $10 used in the previous example. Your gross margin will be 40 percent of sales. Your breakeven level of sales will be:

$$\frac{\$50,000}{.40} = \$125,000$$

If your markup is 66.7 percent rather than 100 percent on cost, you will need to have $125,000 in sales to break even. Moreover, if you want to know the level of sales it will take to generate a $10,000 profit, then the following calculation will tell you:

$$\frac{\$50,000 + \$10,000}{.40} = \$150,000$$

This calculation indicates that with a gross margin of 40 percent of sales, for every dollar past the breakeven point, you generate 40 cents in profit, instead of the 50 cents that would come with a 50 percent gross margin. The question of course remains, Which pricing strategy will be more effective? Will the percentage decrease in price (having a smaller markup) produce an even greater percentage increase in the number of units sold? This is what is known as the "elasticity" equation. If you believe that by lowering the price by 16.7 percent (lowering your price from $10.00 to $8.33) you can increase the number of units sold by more than 16.7 percent, then you should lower your price. If you are right, you will generate a higher level of profit. This assumes, however, that your competition doesn't lower prices or that people will buy more at a lower price.

Example 2: Varying Your Fixed Expenses

Suppose your markup is 100 percent on cost but that your fixed expenses are $55,000 rather than the $50,000 used earlier because you chose a better location to rent. Your new breakeven point will be:

$$\frac{\$55,000}{.50} = \$110,000$$

The question then is, "Will I be able to generate at least $10,000 more in sales to justify the better location?" If the answer is no, then you will probably be better off at the first location. The second location may have had some appeal, but the calculations show that it may not be better in its ability to produce profits.

The increase in fixed expenses associated with this example will also have an impact on the level of sales required to generate a $10,000 profit:

$$\frac{\$55,000 + \$10,000}{.50} = \$130,000$$

Example 3: Combining the Lower Markup With a More Expensive Location

If your cost of goods sold is 60 percent rather than 50 percent of sales and your fixed expenses are expected to be $55,000 rather than $50,000, your breakeven point will be:

$$\frac{\$55,000}{.40} = \$137,500$$

You can see that both your markup and fixed expenses have a direct and considerable effect on the level of sales it will take to break even or to make a profit.

The original example is helpful in determining your breakeven point in sales for the typical year of operation. The first year, however, is not the typical year. It also includes various expenses associated with setting up your business, such as grand opening advertising and decorating. These expenses would not take place in the second or third year. Consequently, you would need to add these to your selling and administrative expenses when figuring your first year's breakeven and profit projections.

You should also note that the total purchase price for equipment should not be treated as an expense in the first year. This is because equipment will be "depreciated," or charged as an expense over the number of years the equipment is expected to be useful. Cost-volume-profit analysis is not the same as cashflow analysis, which will be discussed in the next section.

Cost-volume-profit analysis is particularly helpful for answering the following four questions about your business:

Level 1: What level of sales is necessary to
cover my out-of-pocket expenses?

Fixed expenses are expected to be $40,000, and the contribution margin is expected to be 50 percent of sales.

$$\frac{\$40,000}{.50} = \$80,000$$

Level 2: What level of sales is necessary to
cover my out-of-pocket expenses and pay
me for my time?

You are the sole proprietor. Your salary or "draw" will be what is left over after all the business expenses are paid. You desire $15,000 for your time and effort.

$$\frac{\$40,000 + \$15,000}{.50} = \$110,000$$

Level 3: What level of sales is necessary to
cover my out-of-pocket expenses and my
time, and retire the debt incurred to finance
the business?

You estimate that you will need to borrow $20,000 to supplement what you plan to invest from your personal savings to start the business. If the loan is amortized (treated like a mortgage, with monthly payments covering the interest and principal) over five years, then the annual debt retirement payments will total $5220.

$$\frac{\$40,000 + \$15,000 + \$5220}{.50} = \$120,440$$

Level 4: What level of sales is necessary to
cover my out-of-pocket expenses and my
time, retire the debt, and earn a fair return
on the money invested in the business?

You plan to invest $20,000 in your business and desire a 15 percent ($3000) return on your investment.

$$\frac{\$40,000 + \$15,000 + \$5220 + \$3000}{.50} = \$126,440$$

You may be willing to live with Level 1 for the first year if you financed the business yourself and did not need to borrow any money.

However, if other people invested in the business or if you borrowed money, then the business will have to do better if it is to meet the investor's or lender's expectations. They will want to know before they put money into the business when and if the business will be able to stand on its own feet and pay everyone involved for their time, risk, and money.

Cost-volume-profit analysis may provide a quick estimate of your breakeven point as well as profit and loss levels; but two things need to be stressed. First, your calculations will only be as accurate as your estimates of expenses. Second, when the level of sales increases to a certain point, your selling and administrative expenses (advertising, space, employees, etc.) may also increase. Increases in these expenses will need to be reflected in your calculations.

Both of the examples have been fairly simplistic. Fortunately, computer software known as "electronic spreadsheets," such as Lotus 1-2-3, are available today for handling these and more complicated financial calculations. If your sales estimate for the first year will provide a sufficient level of profit (or an acceptable minimal loss) for you to still be interested in starting the proposed business, then you are ready to work on the remaining parts of your financial plan.

Cashflow Projections

The section on estimating your initial capital requirement emphasized the need to have enough money to start your business as well as to meet expansion or financing needs during the first year of operation. Your cashflow schedule tries to identify when cash will be received from sales and when it will need to be disbursed. The cashflow projections may also be helpful for getting a more accurate estimate of your initial capital requirement.

Your sales forecast for the year may not reflect seasonal fluctuations in sales, when principal payments on your loan may be due, when you will have to pay for replacing the inventory you sell, quarterly insurance payments, etc. The cashflow schedule projects the amounts and timing of cash receipts and disbursements from the time you start ordering your initial inventory, signs, equipment, and so on, to the end of your first year of operation.

The cashflow schedule is particularly important if you have to prepay for some of your assets or expenses. It is also important if you allow your customers to put their purchases "on account." If you expect to have accounts receivable, then you will have to replace your inventory, pay your rent, and so on, out of the business's funds while waiting for your customers to pay what they owe your business.

The cashflow projection identifies periods when you will not have enough money on hand to meet your obligations. The cashflow schedule should give you enough lead time to set up a line of credit with a bank to cover any projected shortages of cash. Conversely, it will identify periods when you may have more cash than you need. If you know this in advance, then you may be able to put it in an interest-bearing account or take advantage of cash discounts with suppliers.

The lack of balance between disbursements and receipts may cause considerable anxiety and adversity. Quite a few businesses with profit potential go bankrupt because they are unable to meet their financial obligations. Their cash obligations were due early in their first year and their sales did not come in time to cover the obligations. Too many business tombstones display the saying, "The owner went to the well; but it was dry!" In business, it is difficult to get instant cash. You need to plan ahead and have enough cash available when you need it.

Preparing Your Pro Forma Financial Statements

You have come a long way on preparing your financial plan. You have estimated: (1) your first year's sales, (2) your breakeven point, (3) your initial capital requirement, (4) whether you have enough money to start your business, and (5) your cashflow statement. (See Table 8-1.) You still need to prepare: (1) your opening day balance sheet, (2) a projected income statement for the first year, (3) the closing balance sheet for the first year, (4) the income statements for the following two to four years, and (5) the balance sheets for the following two to four years. You should also compute the key financial ratios for the first few years of business.

At this point you are probably saying, "Do I really need to do all of these calculations and projections? I doubt that many people going into business do all of these things." You are right; most people starting a business don't perform these computations. Remember, most people fail. They either do not know how to perform the calculations or they are so eager to start their businesses they are unwilling to take the time to look before they leap.

If you want to start a business that beats the odds, then you must do a thorough job of financial planning. This is an essential part of your business plan. These projections not only give you an idea of what you can expect, they also serve as benchmarks to verify whether things are going as planned after the business is started. Would you like to be a passenger on a plane if the pilot did not check the weather report, fuel level, and file a

Table 8-1. First Year's Projected Cashflow Statement

	January	February	March	April
Beginning balance	$40,000	$ 8,569	$ 7,119	$ 6,644
Cash receipts:				
Sales	0	6,000	8,000	9,000
Total cash	$40,000	$14,569	$15,119	$15,644
Cash payments:				
Payroll	2,200	2,200	2,200	2,200
Rent	734	734	734	734
Advertising	1,215	405	405	405
Delivery	130	25	30	35
Supplies	22	22	22	22
Telephone	50	50	50	50
Utilities	67	67	67	67
Insurance	126	0	0	126
Payroll taxes and outlays	292	292	292	292
Licenses	100	0	0	0
Credit card charges	0	60	80	90
Maintenance	20	20	20	20
Legal and accounting	450	100	100	100
Miscellaneous	40	40	40	40
Other	200	0	0	0
Fixtures and equipment	4,000	0	0	0
Installation	200	0	0	0
Decorating	3,000	0	0	0
Inventory	18,000	3,000	4,000	4,500
Deposits	150	0	0	0
Loan payments	435	435	435	435
Total cash payments	$31,431	$ 7,450	$ 8,475	$ 9,116
Minimum cash required	5,000	5,000	5,000	5,000
Cash over (short)	$ 3,569	$ 2,119	$ 1,644	$ 1,528

flight plan before taking off? If not, then do not take the same type of risk by not identifying the key financial factors, projections, and indicators that must be addressed when starting and managing a successful business.

The following pro forma statements will be helpful as you plan your business. Also, if you plan to borrow money from a bank or sell stock to finance your business, then you will be expected to have them.

Preparing Your Initial Balance Sheet

The opening day balance sheet provides a picture of how the business will be financed and where the money will be allocated. The balance

Table 8-1. First Year's Projected Cashflow Statement (*Continued*)

	May	June	July	August
Beginning balance	$ 6,528	$ 6,783	$ 7,528	$ 8,387
Cash receipts:				
Sales	9,500	10,500	11,000	11,500
Total cash	$16,028	$17,283	$18,528	$19,887
Cash payments:				
Payroll	2,200	2,200	2,200	2,200
Rent	734	734	734	734
Advertising	405	405	405	405
Delivery	35	35	40	45
Supplies	22	22	22	22
Telephone	50	50	50	50
Utilities	67	67	67	67
Insurance	0	0	126	0
Payroll taxes and outlays	292	292	292	292
Licenses	0	0	0	0
Credit card charges	95	105	110	115
Maintenance	20	20	20	20
Legal and accounting	100	100	100	100
Miscellaneous	40	40	40	40
Other	0	0	0	0
Fixtures and equipment	0	0	0	0
Installation	0	0	0	0
Decorating	0	0	0	0
Inventory	4,750	5,250	5,500	5,750
Deposits	0	0	0	0
Loan payments	435	435	435	435
Total cash payments	$ 9,245	$ 9,755	$10,141	$10,275
Minimum cash required	5,000	5,000	5,000	5,000
Cash over (short)	$ 1,783	$ 2,528	$ 3,387	$ 4,612

sheet is comprised of assets, liabilities, and net worth (see Table 8-2). Assets represent the items you need to have to operate your business. You will need cash, inventory, equipment, and so on, to sell products or services.

When you start your business, every dollar of assets will have to be financed via debt or money you and other people invest in your business. This is why it is called a "balance" sheet. Every dollar in assets will have to be "balanced" by a dollar of liabilities or equity. The balance sheet is based on the following formula:

$$Assets = liabilities + net\ worth$$

Table 8-1. First Year's Projected Cashflow Statement (*Continued*)

	September	October	November	December
Beginning balance	$ 9,612	$10,837	$11,691	$12,431
Cash receipts:				
Sales	11,500	11,000	10,500	9,500
Total cash	$21,112	$21,837	$22,191	$21,931
Cash payments:				
Payroll	2,200	2,200	2,200	2,200
Rent	734	734	734	734
Advertising	405	405	405	405
Delivery	45	45	40	35
Supplies	22	22	22	22
Telephone	50	50	50	50
Utilities	67	67	67	67
Insurance	0	126	0	0
Payroll taxes and outlays	292	292	292	292
Licenses	0	0	0	0
Credit card charges	115	110	105	95
Maintenance	20	20	20	20
Legal and accounting	100	100	100	100
Miscellaneous	40	40	40	40
Other	0	0	0	0
Fixtures and equipment	0	0	0	0
Installation	0	0	0	0
Decorating	0	0	0	0
Inventory	5,750	5,500	5,250	4,750
Deposits	0	0	0	0
Loan payments	435	435	435	435
Total cash payments	$10,275	$10,146	$ 9,760	$ 9,245
Minimum cash required	5,000	5,000	5,000	5,000
Cash over (short)	$ 5,837	$ 6,691	$ 7,431	$ 7,686

For example, if you plan to start a business with $18,000 of inventory, then the $18,000 will have to come from (or be balanced by) a loan or money from you or other investors.

Net worth or owner's equity represents the portion of business assets owned by you and other investors. If your business is profitable, you will be in a position to expand the business (increase assets) or pay off the loans used to finance some of the original assets.

The initial balance sheet is important for numerous reasons. It indicates how much money will be needed to start the business. It also gives bankers and investors an idea about what will be owned and what will be owed. The balance sheet also provides a picture of whether the assets will comprise inventory, fixtures, or land and buildings. Some assets

Table 8-2. Projected Opening Day Balance Sheet

February 1st, Year 1	
Assets	
Cash	$ 8,569
Prepaid insurance	42
Inventory	18,000
Equipment	4,000
Less accumulated depreciation of equipment	(95)
Deposits with utilities	100
Total assets	$30,616
Liabilities	
Long-term notes payable	$19,749
Owner's equity	$10,867
Total liabilities and owner's equity	$30,616

are easier to convert to cash than others if the business falters. The balance sheet thereby indicates the downside risk for potential lenders and investors.

Preparing the First Calendar-Year-End Income Statement

The income statement reflects the results of the year's business activity. It indicates the level of sales, the cost of goods sold, operating expenses, and the resulting profit or loss. If you prepared the cashflow statement, then most of the work for projecting the first year's income statement is already done. The income statement for the first year is important because it projects the level of profit available for funding growth, reducing debt obligations, or providing a return that includes dividends for the investors. Because of uncertainty of the first year's sales, it may be advisable to prepare your first year's income statement for three different levels of sales: the most likely level, a pessimistic level, and an optimistic level. (See Table 8-3.)

If the projected income statement indicates that the business is expected to make a profit in the first year, then the owner must be prepared to pay income taxes. For this and other reasons, it may be advisable to figure income statements on a monthly basis for the first year. The Internal Revenue Service and your state's department of revenue

Table 8-3. Projected First Year's Income Statement

	Pessimistic	Most Likely	Optimistic
Sales	$ 86,400	$108,000	$130,000
Cost of goods sold	43,200	54,000	65,000
Gross margin	$ 43,200	$ 54,000	$ 65,000
Less expenses:			
Payroll	26,400	26,400	26,400
Rent	8,808	8,808	8,808
Advertising	6,075	6,075	6,075
Delivery	432	540	648
Supplies	264	264	264
Telephone	500	600	700
Utilities	800	800	800
Insurance	504	504	560
Payroll taxes	3,504	3,504	3,504
Licenses	100	100	100
Credit card charges	860	1,080	1,300
Maintenance	240	240	240
Legal and accounting	1,550	1,550	1,550
Miscellaneous	480	480	480
Depreciation	1,140	1,140	1,140
Installation	200	200	200
Other	200	200	200
Decorating	3,000	3,000	3,000
Total selling and administrative exp.	$ 55,057	$ 55,485	$ 55,969
Net profit from operations	$(11,857)	$ (1,485)	$ 9,031
Less interest expense	2,043	2,043	2,043
Net profit before taxes	$(13,900)	$ (3,528)	$ 6,988
Taxes	-0-	-0-	1,362
Net income after taxes	$(13,900)	$ (3,528)	$ 5,626

will expect estimated income tax payments on a quarterly and, in some cases, monthly basis when you start making a profit. The income statement will enable you to identify when to expect to generate a profit, how much it will be, what your tax obligations will be, and when you will need to have funds available to meet your tax obligations.

Another tax factor should also be noted. The Internal Revenue Service wants small businesses to use the calendar year for tax returns. If you start your business in May, your first year's projected income statement should reflect your expected levels of sales, expenses, and profit or loss for that calendar year, even though it may not be for 12 months.

Table 8-4. Projected First Year's Ending Balance Sheet

December 31, Year 1	
Assets	
Cash	$12,686
Prepaid insurance	0
Inventory	18,000
Equipment	4,000
Less accumulated depreciation of equipment	(1,140)
Deposits with utilities	100
Total assets	$33,646
Liabilities	
Notes payable	$16,825
Owner's equity	$16,821
Total liabilities and owner's equity	$33,646

Preparing Your First Calendar-Year-End Balance Sheet

It will be beneficial for you to project the balance sheet for the completion of your first calendar year of operation. This balance sheet will reflect the "change" in financial condition from the initial balance sheet resulting from your cashflow and profit or loss. Unless you added more debt or investment capital during the first year, most of the changes between these two balance sheets will be reflected in the income statement.

If your business is expected to make a profit and have a positive cashflow, your assets and equity should increase. Conversely, if the business is expected to lose money and there is not expected to be enough cash available to meet financial obligations, you may need to seek additional debt or equity financing to provide a sufficient level of cash to continue operations.

In any event, the first calendar-year-end balance sheet will provide a picture of the amount of assets involved in the business as well as the extent to which they are owned versus owed. In most cases, if the business made a profit, your balance sheet will indicate that you own a larger portion of the business than when you first opened your doors. (See Table 8-4.)

Preparing the Income Statements for the Second Through Fifth Years

It is advisable to prepare income statements for at least the first three years of operation. The second and third years are particularly important. As noted earlier, most businesses do not make a profit in their first year. By protecting your second- and third-year income statements, you will have a better idea about whether you will be profitable, when you may achieve profitability, as well as the level of profit or loss you may expect each year (see Table 8-5).

Your sales estimate represents the most important part of your projected income statements. You will need to forecast whether your sales will increase from year to year. Many businesses experience a continued increase in sales from the first to second year of operation. While you will be continuing your effort to create more new customers in the second year, you may already benefit from repeat customers from the first year. It is for this reason that you should forecast your second year's income statement on a quarterly basis.

The quarterly income statements should reflect any growth in sales as

Table 8-5. Projected Income Statements for the Second and Third Years

	Year 2	Year 3
Sales	$125,000	$137,500
Cost of goods sold	62,500	68,750
Gross margin	$ 62,500	$ 68,750
Less expenses:		
Payroll	27,720	29,106
Rent	10,000	11,000
Advertising	5,625	6,188
Delivery	650	725
Supplies	270	280
Telephone	650	730
Utilities	830	860
Insurance	560	600
Payroll taxes	3,660	3,842
Licenses	100	100
Credit card charges	1,250	1,375
Maintenance	240	240
Legal and accounting	1,550	1,550
Miscellaneous	480	480
Depreciation	815	584
Decorating	500	1,000
Total selling and administrative expenses	$ 54,900	$ 58,660
Net profit from operations	7,600	10,090
Less interest expense	1,675	1,266
Net profit before taxes	$ 5,925	$ 8,824
Taxes	1,158	1,728
Net income after taxes	$ 4,767	$ 7,096

well as any seasonality for your business. The quarterly income statements will also be helpful if you want to project your cashflow for your second year of operation. The quarterly statements may then be consolidated into the income statement for your second year. The second year's income statement will also be important if your business will be operating on a calendar year. If you plan to start your business in May, then your first year's income statement may only reflect eight months of business. Your second year's income statement is important because it will reflect the complete business cycle from January through December.

It is worth your time and effort to project the income statements for the fourth and fifth years. (See Table 8-6.) They do not need to be done

Table 8-6. Projected Income Statements for the Fourth and Fifth Years

	Year 4	Year 5
Sales	$158,250	$172,250
Cost of goods sold	79,125	86,125
Gross margin	$ 79,125	$ 86,125
Less expenses:		
Payroll	40,761	42,800
Rent	14,000	15,500
Advertising	7,121	7,751
Delivery	791	861
Supplies	395	430
Telephone	791	860
Utilities	1,200	1,250
Insurance	920	980
Payroll taxes	6,114	6,240
Licenses	120	120
Credit card charges	1,582	1,722
Maintenance	320	340
Legal and accounting	1,550	1,550
Depreciation	1,711	1,386
Installation	300	0
Decorating	3,000	500
Total selling and administrative expenses	$ 80,676*	$ 82,290
Net profit from operations	$ (1,551)	$ 3,835
Less interest expense	$ 808	$ 298
Net profit before taxes	$ (2,359)	$ 3,537
Taxes	0	690
Net income after taxes	$ (2,359)	$ 2,847

*Reflects an additional part-time employee, a larger facility, decorating, and the purchase of more fixtures.

on a quarterly basis unless your business will have wide seasonal fluctuations in sales. The third through fifth year's income statements will provide a picture of the projected level of business activity and profits. If you borrowed money to start the business, then the loan officer will want to see if the business will be making enough money to pay off the note in five years. The people who put money into the business will also want to know what they can expect in return for their investment.

The third through fifth year's income statements will also be important because they should indicate whether you expect the business to level off or continue growing. If your business plan involves opening an additional store, offering additional goods or services, or expanding your sales territory, then your projected income statements should reflect these changes. The projected income statements should indicate the resulting increases in sales, expenses, and profits.

The projected income statements will be based on numerous assumptions. You will have to estimate the rate of inflation, the nature and extent of competition, and whether your target markets are expected to grow, stay about the same, or decline. Computerized spreadsheets may make it easier to do the financial projections, but you will have to give a lot of thought to what the future may hold, who your competitors will be, and what your business should be doing in the years to come.

Preparing the Balance Sheets for the Second Through Fifth Years

The projected income statements will enable you to prepare the projected balance sheets beyond the first year of operation. (See Tables 8-7 and 8-8.) The projected income statements will indicate the level of profits projected for each year. Each year's profit or loss will affect the corresponding year's balance sheet. Profits enable the business to pay off its debts and increase the percentage of the business's assets that are owned rather than owed.

The balance sheets will also reflect the extent to which various assets are being depreciated. If you bought a piece of equipment for $5000 that had a useful life of five years, then each year's balance sheet will reflect the declining, or "depreciated," value of that asset. The balance sheet thereby indicates the "book" value of the business's assets.

The balance sheets represent "pictures" of what the business is expected to look like at the close of each calendar year. Each balance sheet will show the size and composition of the assets, the liabilities and debts, as well as the net worth of the business to its owners. The balance sheet

Table 8-7. Projected Second- and Third-Year-End Balance Sheets

	December 31, Year 2	December 31, Year 3
Assets		
Cash	$12,916	$14,992
Inventory	20,833	22,917
Equipment	4,000	4,000
Less accumulated depreciation of equipment	(1,955)	(2,539)
Deposits with utilities	100	100
Total assets	$35,894	$39,470
Liabilities		
Quarterly income taxes payable	$ 290	$ 432
Notes payable	13,282	9,330
Total liabilities	$13,572	$ 9,762
Owner's equity	$22,322	$29,708
Total liabilities and owner's equity	$35,894	$39,470

Table 8-8. Projected Fourth- and Fifth-Year-End Balance Sheets

	December 31, Year 4	December 31, Year 5
Assets		
Cash	$17,036	$31,225
Inventory	26,375	28,708
Equipment	8,000	8,000
Less accumulated depreciation of equipment	(4,250)	(5,636)
Deposits with utilities	100	100
Total assets	$47,261	$62,397
Liabilities		
Quarterly income taxes payable	$ 0	$ 173
Notes payable	4,920	0
Total liabilities	$ 4,920	$ 173
Owner's equity	$42,341	$62,224
Total liabilities and owner's equity	$47,261	$62,397

will also reflect whether the business will need to borrow money, or if some of its profits can be distributed to the owners.

The balance sheet for the fifth year will be particularly relevant if you signed a five-year note to help start the business. The fifth year's balance sheet will indicate what your business will look like in financial terms. If you have not borrowed any additional money and have the cash to retire the five-year note when it comes due, then you will own the whole business. When people start a business and get a loan, five years may seem like a long time, but your financial projections let you see if there will be "light at the end of the five-year tunnel." The notion of owning the business at the end of five years offers an exciting prospect and will make the time, effort, and anxiety associated with starting a new business more worthwhile.

Running the Numbers Is an Essential Part of the Business Plan

This part of the business plan can be viewed as a "financial" roadmap for charting the future direction of your business. A considerable amount of time will have to be spent in analyzing your business and making the financial calculations. These activities are an essential part of your business plan. Few people who start a business have an in-depth understanding of financial accounting. Nevertheless, this is an area of starting and managing a business that cannot be ignored or left to an accountant. Almost every business decision has a financial dimension. If the number-one reason for small business failure is mismanagement and the number-two reason is financial problems, then you need to increase your chances for beating the odds by developing your competency in this area.

PART 3

The ABCs of Financing and Alternatives to Starting From Scratch

9

Applying for a Loan

Few People Have All the Money They Need

If you find you do not have enough money to start your business, don't give up. When most people compute their initial capital requirement, they find that they do not have enough money to start their business. There are numerous avenues available for providing external financing for your business.

Quite a few businesses start as partnerships because the person who wanted to start the business did not have enough money and was therefore willing to share the ownership to see the business come alive. Another approach for securing additional funding is to start your business as a corporation. As a corporation, you can sell stock to people who want to invest in your business. Venture capital firms also buy stock in businesses. However, they rarely buy stock in a new business until it has demonstrated high-growth potential. Venture capitalists should not be considered for initial capital financing.

One of the most common ways to finance a business start-up is to borrow money. Borrowing from an individual or a financial institution, as with partnerships and corporations, has advantages and drawbacks. The primary advantage to borrowing is that you do not dilute the ownership of the business. Lenders are creditors, not owners. Another advantage is that interest payments are tax-deductible as a business expense. When a business pays dividends to shareholders as a return on their investment, they are not treated as tax deductions.

The major disadvantage with borrowing money is that if you are unable to meet your loan obligations, your business could be in jeopardy. If you fail to make your loan payments, the lender can initiate legal action to seize the assets financed by the loan. Foreclosure can result in the liquidation of your business. When a business is liquidated, government agencies and creditors are at the front of the line when the business's assets are converted into cash. You and any partners or shareholders will be at the end of the line. The "owners" of the business get the "table scraps," if any exist, when the liquidation is completed.

Quite a few businesses start with money borrowed from friends or relatives. These people are often referred to as "angels" to small businesses. Using angels may permit some flexibility, a lower interest rate, and less paperwork than borrowing from a financial institution. However, financing via friends or relatives has at least two major drawbacks. First, these individuals may need their money before you or they expected. One of the advantages of bank financing is that as long as your business is operating within mutually agreed guidelines, banks will not request their money before it is due. Second, you may be jeopardizing your friendship and family goodwill. When friends and family lend people money, relationships tend to change. Instead of being asked, "How are you?" they will ask, "How's the business doing?" When you borrow money from friends and relatives, it rarely strengthens those relationships. Moreover, they may not be willing or able to lend you the money anyway.

When all is said and done, many people starting a business choose to borrow money from a financial institution. Numerous types of financial institutions lend businesses money. Insurance companies lend money, but they usually deal with existing businesses seeking millions of dollars. Small business investment companies (SBICs) provide long-term debt and equity funding, but they tend to favor existing businesses that plan to expand rather than those that are starting operations. Investment banking firms also provide debt financing, but their expectations are similar to venture capital firms. They are interested in businesses that have the potential to at least double or triple in size each year. Few new businesses have that potential.

In ancient times it was said that all roads lead to Rome. Today, most roads for people needing to borrow money to start a business lead to a bank. Banks are the primary commercial lender for business start-ups. You may have heard someone criticize banks because, "They will lend you money only if you don't need it!" This is not necessarily true. Banks are in the business of lending money. However, banks make their money by lending it to people who pay their loans with interest. If you know someone who applied for a loan to start a business and was turned down, that bank determined that the risk of default outweighed their expected interest income. Banks recognize that risk is part of any business proposition, but they are very cautious when it comes to lending their depositors' money. They know most start-ups fail, especially start-ups by first-timers.

If you are interested in borrowing money from a bank, then you must be able to demonstrate to the bank's loan officer or loan committee that your new business will generate a reasonable profit with only minimal risk. A good way to prepare for applying for a loan is to know the criteria that loan officers use when they review loan requests. Loan officers tend to evaluate a loan request for start-up financing according to what are commonly called the "six C's" of commercial lending.

The Six C's of Commercial Lending

The First C: Your "Character"

The first and foremost thing loan officers look for when reviewing a loan proposal is evidence of your trustworthiness. This is crucial. If there is anything in your background that indicates any lack of integrity, loan officers will usually reject your loan application without even reviewing your proposed business idea.

Loan applications usually include a section which permits the bank to initiate a thorough credit check on you. Banks place a premium on integrity because they will rely on your statements about your business and the corresponding financial projections. If your financial, professional, or personal background has any significant blemishes, then your chances for borrowing money from a bank are diminished.

If your business is to be a proprietorship or a partnership, the bank will not be lending the *business* money. From a legal point of view, the bank is lending *you* the money. Both you and your business plan have to measure up to the bank's standards. Even if you start your business as a corporation, the bank will still want to check out the principal officers and directors for the business. In any event, be prepared to identify all the people who will be an important part of your new business. In baseball, when you get three strikes, you are out. In commercial lending, the lack of integrity almost automatically means you are out!

The Second C: Your "Capability" to Manage the Business

Banks know that mismanagement is the number-one reason for new business failure. Your loan proposal must demonstrate that you and everyone else who will be making the various decisions which are part of starting and operating a new business know what you are doing. Banks are more likely to lend money to a business that will be managed by someone who has extensive business experience, particularly in the type of business being proposed. Loan officers are very reluctant to lend money to first-timers who may be using a trial-and-error approach to managing.

Loan officers want to know the professional background and success of the owner and manager of the new venture. They want to know the levels of experience and relevant education for each person involved in running the business. Your loan proposal should indicate how each person is suited for his or her position. Your loan request should include a biographical sketch and a résumé for each key person.

A rule of thumb to remember is that if you have limited experience in the field, then your chances of getting a loan are also limited. This is why banks may look more favorably on a first-timer who is starting as a franchisee rather than as an independent business. Most well-respected franchises: (1) are selective in who they allow to acquire franchise rights, (2) offer training to key people before the business opens, and (3) provide management assistance on a regular basis.

If you lack relevant experience, you should consider going the franchise route, gaining the experience by working for a similar business, or hiring someone to manage your business who already has a proven track record. You could also consider bringing in a partner instead of hiring a manager, if the partner has the appropriate experience. In any event, bankers know that there is a direct relationship between previous experience and new business success.

The Third C: Your Business's "Capacity" to Pay Off the Note

Banks operate under the very simple rule: "We make money only if we lend to businesses that make money." If the loan officer feels comfortable with your personal background and your ability to exercise good judgment when making business decisions, then the officer's attention will be directed to the extent to which your business will be able to make a profit.

The financial part of your business plan will be an integral part of your loan proposal. Your financial projections will provide the type of data the loan officer will need to review your business idea. Loan officers will be particularly interested in: (1) how soon you can generate a positive cashflow, (2) when you will show a profit, (3) how large it will be, (4) whether it will be lasting, and (5) whether various assets will be financed via debt or equity. You should be prepared to present the cashflow projections for at least the first two years, and the balance sheets from day 1 through the first three to five years.

The loan officer will be looking for the business's ability to pay all financial obligations. This individual will be particularly interested in the business's ability to pay the monthly interest (and in some cases, principal) as well as its ability to pay off the note when it comes due. Loan officers frequently remind borrowers, "Sales may pay the interest, but profits are needed to pay the principal." Bank officials look for an early positive cashflow (where receipts exceed disbursements) with profitability to follow soon for debt retirement. The shorter the period of time your business has to rely on external financing, the greater the likelihood of qualifying for a loan.

Your ability to prepare, present, and support your financial projections is an indication of your capability to manage a business. If you have an accountant help you prepare the financial part of the business plan, be sure that you understand the nature and logic of the financial projections. This is one of the reasons why you should have knowledge of accounting and finance. If every time the loan officer asks you a question about the basis for certain figures you respond by saying, "I don't know, you'll have to ask my accountant," you are destined to reduce your chances for getting a loan.

The Fourth C: The "Conditions," or Terms, of the Loan

Even if the loan officer is satisfied with the first three C's, the nature of your loan request will also influence the bank's willingness to lend you money. Your loan request will need to provide answers to the following three questions: (1) How much money are you requesting? (2) What will it be used for? and (3) For how long will it be needed?

The first question has considerable bearing on whether you will get the loan. If your opening day balance sheet shows that you expect more than half of your assets to be financed via a bank loan, you are likely to encounter difficulty. Most loan officers operate with a 50/50 rule. They do not want to put more than one-half the money into your business. If a loan exceeds 50 percent of the initial capital requirement, the business would be more theirs than yours. They are reluctant to risk more money than you are willing to contribute.

Banks expect at least half of the assets to be financed by you or other investors for three reasons. First, they want the owners to be committed to the business. They feel that you will be more responsible if your money is tied to the business's success. Second, if you don't have enough money or are unable to get other investors to commit their money to the business, then why should they put their depositors' money into your business? Bankers feel that if you are unwilling to commit your own money or are unable to convince other individuals to invest in your business, then either your business lacks merit or you lack the selling skills that will be important for your business to succeed.

The third reason bankers do not want to finance more than half the assets is they want to cover themselves if your business fails. When businesses fail, the creditors frequently get to sell (liquidate the business's) assets to recover what the business owes them. Loan officers use the 50/50 rule because, if the business fails, they may still be able to liquidate the assets for 50 cents per dollar of assets. This is their "financial parachute." If they can get 50 cents per dollar of assets, they may be able to recover the amount of the loan's outstanding balance.

As you can see, you and other investors are at the end of the line when the assets are liquidated. Bankers do not like to take excessive risks. They reduce their risks by limiting the amount of the loan to a certain portion of the business's assets, using those assets as security, and being as close as possible to the front of the line to get their money out of the business if it is unable to meet its financial obligations.

The opening day balance sheet also helps answer the second question, "What is the loan to be used for?" The opening day balance sheet indicates: (1) the type and amount of assets your business will have to start operations, (2) the amount of assets financed by debt, and (3) the amount of assets funded by investors. Loan officers want to know if the money you want to borrow will be used to purchase fixtures and equipment, to buy a building, to pay for inventory, to finance your receivables, or to cover your monthly expenses until you have a positive cashflow.

Loan officers prefer to lend money for items that can be identified, can last for a number of years, and can be repossessed and sold if all else fails. If your loan request is for money to pay for your grand opening advertising, rent, and salaries, you may find the bank reluctant to lend money that will disappear quickly. Also, if the other tangible assets are to be leased or specifically financed by the manufacturer or distributor, these businesses may be in front of the bank when the line forms to pick up the pieces if you don't beat the odds.

The third question, "How long a period of time?," is related to the preceding question. The length of the loan is affected by the nature of the assets you are trying to finance. If you are using the loan to buy your inventory, you should not expect a loan for more than a few months. If you plan to use the money to buy equipment, the bank may be willing to lend the money for a couple of years. If you are planning to buy a building, you may be able to secure a loan for at least 10 years.

Loan officers look at the "useful life" of the assets they are financing. They rarely lend money for longer than the assets are expected to last.

Borrowing money is quite different from getting a mortgage to finance the purchase of a house. You will be expected to have a lot of equity up-front. A 5 percent down payment will rarely get a loan officer's attention. Moreover, banks rarely lend money for more than five years unless it is used to finance a building. You may have been able to get a 20- to 30-year mortgage for your home, but you will have to demonstrate to the bank that your business has the ability to pay off the loan within five years.

Two other "conditions" also need to be kept in mind when borrowing from a bank. First, you will have to carry enough insurance on your business's assets so they are covered in the event of a fire or other non-business loss. The bank will also place various restrictive covenants on the operation of your business. You will be expected to provide certain financial records on a regular basis which reflect the financial health of your business. You will need to maintain certain levels of inventory, receivables, and cash. The restrictions may include getting prior approval from the bank if you are thinking of making any major changes in your balance sheet via the sale or purchase of assets or altering the business's equity or debt configuration.

The bank may not technically be a partner in the business, but it may seem to be the "senior partner" in certain instances. Borrowing money involves more than filling in a loan application and shaking hands. It needs to be addressed as a rigorous process. If you approach the bank in a casual manner, the loan officer is likely to: (1) infer that you are not serious about your business, (2) infer that you are unwilling or unable to do your homework, or (3) generalize that you will not be able to make a favorable impression on potential customers. In any of these situations, your chances for getting a loan are minimal.

The Fifth C: The "Context" of Your Proposed Business

No business exists in a vacuum. Most loan officers have their own perceptions and preferences. When lending money for a business start-up, loan officers have to exercise their judgment. Lending is not a science. There are a myriad of factors that have to be considered when sizing up the merit and risk associated with financing a new business.

You need to recognize that loan officers have attitudes about most types of businesses. Some loan officers get excited about manufacturing or high-technology businesses. Other loan officers seem to favor retail or service businesses. This may also be true for banks. Smaller banks tend to be more "retail" oriented. They actively seek opportunities to lend to promising local businesses. Numerous large banks have a reputation for avoiding business start-ups and for not making loans for less than $100,000.

Banks that have had successful lending experiences with certain types of businesses are more open-minded when they review a loan proposal for a similar business. Conversely, some loan officers and banks have had bad experiences with certain types of businesses. If you are planning to start a similar business, you may encounter considerable skepticism by the loan officer.

If the loan officer has extensive experience in your business's field or has had a good track record for lending to that type of business, this may be to your advantage. However, if your idea is very "foreign" to the loan officer or falls into the category of "I'll be darned if I ever lend any money to that kind of business again!" then you may be better off looking for another loan officer or approaching a different bank. Many loan officers are known to avoid lending to restaurants, video rental stores, and women's clothing boutiques.

Expect loan officers to look at the context in which you will start your business. They may pay particular attention to potential economic, legal, employee, supplier, or environmental problems. You may have financial projections to demonstrate your business's "capacity" to pay off the loan. However, loan officers place a premium on the local, regional, and national economic picture. Their feeling about whether there will be inflation, a recession, tight money, high unemployment, etc., will influence your likelihood of getting a loan. Loan officers can get "cold feet" about lending in general, and new business start-ups in particular, if the overall economic outlook is not good. Even though your target area may have growth potential, loan officers may still have "cool feet." If your type of business is recession-proof and inflation-proof, then you may be in good shape.

Loan officers are also interested in whether your business is competition-proof and obsolescence-proof. They will be particularly interested in whether the market is already saturated—too many businesses competing for too few customers. They will also be interested in whether you will be competing with chains and franchises or if you will be up against small independent businesses. Loan officers tend to look more favorably on your business plan if: (1) you have a fairly new product or service that people already want to buy, (2) there is little competition, (3) the competition is made up of small independent businesses, and (4) few businesses of your type have failed. Loan officers don't seem to be bothered if other similar businesses are starting as much as when similar businesses are starting to fail. They prefer the situation where a growing opportunity exists, even with competition, than one where the market is already showing signs that it is waning.

Loan officers frequently contact their headquarters to learn about the success rates for certain types of business. The bank's staff at its headquarters usually has access to trade data as well as the track record for similar businesses in their loan portfolios.

Loan officers also look at the ease with which other people can start your type of business. If your type of business requires extensive experience, rigorous licensing requirements, and considerable capital, then the bank will be more willing to lend you money if you are one of only a few people who meet all the qualifications. Conversely, if almost anyone could start your type of business with no experience and a minimal investment, then this would be disconcerting to a loan officer.

Legal issues also concern loan officers. Certain businesses have come under closer scrutiny and regulation in recent years. Billboard businesses have encountered considerable regulation in many towns. Some municipalities have passed ordinances requiring billboard businesses to reduce the number and size of their signs. Some towns have gone so far as to require that all billboards be removed within the decade. Day-care, exercise, pest control, and other businesses are expected to encounter additional licensing requirements and regulations in the years to come.

If your business is expected to have numerous employees, then the loan officer may be concerned about the likelihood of unionization. The potential for a strike can give a loan officer cool feet. The potential for employee accidents and the business's liability may also affect the loan officer.

The loan officer may be concerned about your vulnerability to suppliers. Numerous small businesses fail because their suppliers went out of business or failed to continue providing for the needs of those businesses. Restrictive covenants between one of your competitors and a supplier to not provide service to your business may be illegal, but informal "practices" continue in many fields.

The ability to get insurance coverage is another area that concerns businesses and loan officers. Insurance premiums for some businesses have more than tripled in the last couple of years. Some businesses have had to reduce their coverage or go without coverage because the costs have increased so much. A few businesses have even closed their doors because they could not get insurance coverage. Some of these businesses did not have a checkered past. The insurance companies simply decided to discontinue coverage to that kind of business. Neither you nor your loan officer wants your business to die on the vine because you cannot get what you need to do business. The greater the risk of nonsupply, the greater the likelihood the loan officer will not approve your loan request.

Environmental factors may also make the loan officer apprehensive about financing your business. If your business can be adversely affected by the weather, then the loan officer may not want to risk the bank's depositors' money. Loan officers like to finance businesses that are influenced by their managers rather than by mother nature. Loan officers also tend to shy away from any business that could be involved in any type of ecological disaster. If your business will be dealing with anything that is flammable or toxic, or has the potential to be a pollutant, then the loan officer may steer clear of your proposal.

The fifth C indicates that your loan proposal can be rejected because of the nature and context of your business, regardless of the strength of the other C's. In such a case, you will have to provide even more documentation in your business plan and loan request to substantiate your optimism and demonstrate the viability of your business idea. For this reason, it may be advisable to set up an appointment with your bank's commercial loan officer when you are in the early stages of preparing your business plan. You may be able to get an initial impression of the loan officer's interest in such a business. You may find that the bank has adopted a policy of not lending to that type of business. Hopefully, you will find the loan officer to be enthusiastic about your idea. If so, the loan officer may be able to get or recommend some sources of data to help you prepare your business plan and loan request. You may find that the officer may be able to provide considerable assistance. This may pay off later. The more the bank helps you from the beginning, the more likely it will approve your loan request.

The Sixth C: Your "Collateral"

Most people who apply for a start-up loan place too much emphasis on their collateral. Your collateral is important, but loan officers do not put it at the top of their criteria when reviewing a loan request. Loan officers want to finance businesses that will make money. If they have reservations about potential profitability, then a large amount of collateral may be required to cover their risk. Nevertheless, banks tend to operate with the policy, "If it takes a lot of collateral to cover the bank's position, then don't approve the loan."

If your business is unable to meet its loan obligations, then the bank is placed in a couple of awkward situations. First, the loan officer has to admit to not exercising good judgment by lending you the money. Second, the officer has to go through the process of converting assets into cash to recover the bank's money. This takes time and diverts the bank from what it is in business to do. It also does little to develop goodwill with your employees, investors, suppliers, and creditors.

Your loan request will need to reflect what assets can be used as collateral for the bank loan. If your business is to be a proprietorship or partnership, the bank will probably ask you to include personal balance sheets for you and any partners. Remember, you are the business. If it fails to meet its obligations to the bank, the bank will look to your personal assets for settlement of the loan. If your business will be set up as a corporation, don't be surprised if the bank and other creditors ask you and the other major stockholders to provide personal balance sheets. The bank may also expect you and the other major stockholders to personally cosign the loan. This will create the same personal financial obligation as if the business was formed as a proprietorship or partnership.

Your collateral represents a "financial parachute" for the bank. Hopefully, it will never have to be used. As with parachutes, the bank will look for collateral that is large enough to break the fall. Banks also prefer collateral that can be easily converted to cash. If your business's collateral will be custom manufacturing equipment that may be difficult to resell and has minimal value once used, then your banker may place little value on your collateral. The same may also be true if your personal collateral is a 200-acre family-owned farm in Kansas.

Collateral may be one of the six C's, but it rarely makes up for a weakness in any of the other five C's. You will need to provide enough collateral to reduce the downside risk for banks, but don't treat collateral as the primary selling point of your loan request.

Other Things to Consider
When Applying for a Loan

As you enter into the process of applying for a loan, you should keep in mind the following points: First, it may be worth your time to approach a few banks, not just the one you are using now. Some banks are more receptive to start-up loans than others. Also, loan terms may vary from bank to bank. You may be able to find a lower interest rate, a more flexible payback schedule, or fewer restrictive covenants. Second, be prepared to scale down your request or even your business idea to fit what you can borrow. The 50/50 rule is fairly common.

Third, you may need to do some creative financing. Be prepared to ask your suppliers to help finance your business by providing "trade credit." Trade credit lets you pay off suppliers over a period of time. This may be a necessity. The length of time may be shorter than what a bank may provide, but it could be at a lower rate.

Fourth, if your balance sheet shows that you have a lot of equity in your house, then don't be surprised if the loan officer recommends refinancing your house to get the money you need rather than getting a business loan. In some cases this may be worthwhile. Remember, however, that the bank may prefer selling your home rather than liquidating your business's assets if your business is unable to meet its debt obligations. If the loan officer recommends refinancing your house, give this the amount of thought it deserves.

Fifth, there are alternative sources of financing. The U.S. Small Business Administration may help you get debt financing if you meet its requirements. The SBA is often called the "lender of last resort." The SBA will review your loan request only if it has merit and has been turned down by at least one bank. If you are in a large metropolitan area, you will have to be turned down by at least two banks before you can apply for SBA financing.

The SBA applies the same six C's when reviewing your loan proposal. Moreover, the terms of the loan are not that different from what a bank would have offered you if your loan proposal met the bank's standards in the first place. The irony of an SBA loan is that the SBA actually does not lend the money to you. It guarantees the majority of the loan to the commercial bank that actually lends you the money. For this reason, the SBA cannot operate as a small business welfare agency. The SBA's standards are expected to be even more stringent in the future.

You should also check with your state's department of commerce. Some states have funds set aside for start-ups. If your business has considerable growth potential and technological appeal, federal agencies may be willing to provide financial assistance. For example, the SBA's Small Business Innovation Research Program funds businesses that are involved in high-technology research and development. Some states have similar programs.

When it comes to financing a new business there are many ways to "skin the cat." It is wise to remember that in all cases the cat has to be worth skinning! Your business plan and loan proposal will need to be thorough and reflect the potential for success that will justify the financial risk others will have to take to help you get your business off to a good start. This is an important hurdle in starting a business. Keep in mind that the second reason for small business failure is the lack of capital. If you do not handle this part of starting your business well, you will not have enough money to start your business or you may start it with an insufficient amount of money.

Borrowing money is one of the facts of life when starting and managing a business. In some instances, it may be advisable to borrow money even if you believe you have enough money to finance the venture by yourself. This way you have some of your money on the sidelines or a line of credit from a bank if you need it. The other advantage of borrowing money is that you let someone else's money make money for you. The best of all worlds would be if lenders financed most of your business. You would not have to put much money into the business. When your business eventually paid off its debts, you would get all its profits and own all its assets. When you create and maintain customers for a profit, you will be transforming debt into net worth.

10

Buying an Existing Business

Sometimes It's Better Not to Start From Scratch

So far, this book has focused on starting a new business from scratch. As with most things in life, this approach to getting into business has advantages and drawbacks. The primary advantages of starting from scratch include being able to develop a business to capitalize on a unique opportunity or business idea and having the pleasure of knowing that you did it on your own. The major disadvantage of starting from scratch is that you will need to come up with the answers to the hundreds of questions involved in starting a new business. This may represent a "challenge," but it also represents considerable risk, especially for the first-timer.

A thoroughly prepared business plan still will not provide all the answers nor will it identify all the questions that will need to be addressed. When you start a new business from scratch, you will be engaged in a lot of trial and error. Your business plan is based on assumptions about whether there are customers in search of a business, what will be the appropriate products or services to offer, what advertising will work, and so on. Quite a few of your assumptions will not be right on target. This is why so many start-ups fail.

The business plan will help you be more systematic in analyzing the market. It will also force you to collect data to test the validity of your assumptions. Nevertheless, when the first-timer attempts to start a business from scratch, that person is usually taking the most risky path for going into business.

There are two other ways to go into business. You can buy an existing

166

business or you can acquire the rights to a franchise. Both alternatives offer the opportunity to bypass many of the questions associated with starting a business from scratch. In each case, assumptions about the business idea have already been field-tested.

While these avenues may reduce the likelihood of failure, each comes with a corresponding cost. Moreover, neither approach can guarantee success. This chapter will address the pros and cons of buying an existing business. The next chapter will cover the benefits and drawbacks associated with acquiring a franchise.

Why Buy an Existing Business?

In many instances, it may be advisable to buy an existing business rather than start one from scratch. The greatest benefit of buying an existing business is that it is a tangible entity. When you start a new business from scratch, you have to estimate the levels of sales, costs, and profits. When you consider buying a business, the seller can provide actual financial data that reflects the business's performance. Instead of having faith that people will buy the products and services, you will have a record to review of how many people bought what and when. When you start a business from scratch, you are dealing with an almost endless list of unknowns. When you buy an existing business, one of the things you are also buying is the answers to questions that could not be answered prior to starting a business from scratch.

One of the interesting things about buying a business is that the process is not that different from the process of starting a new venture. First, you need to start by identifying an area where a substantial and lasting opportunity exists. Second, you must have or must develop the capability to cultivate the necessary skills and resources to capitalize on the opportunity. Third, there must be sufficient profit potential or return on the amount of money to be invested in the business to justify the risk.

The first few chapters of this book indicated the need for these three factors to be present and the importance of developing a thorough business plan. It was also noted that getting into a business is not something that can be done overnight. Starting a business from scratch is a very time-consuming process. The same is true for buying an existing business.

While it may take less time to buy a business than to start one, it may still take 4 to 12 months from the time you start looking for opportunities to the transfer of title to the business you buy. It could take more than a year to find one that meets your personal preferences and financial objectives.

The major advantage of buying an existing business is that everything is already in place. Instead of hoping that people will be interested in your new business, you have customers who are accustomed to buying from that business. Instead of contacting and negotiating with suppliers to provide merchandise and trade credit, you get established relationships. Instead of hiring and training people, you get a seasoned group of employees.

There are numerous other potential benefits with buying an existing business. Hopefully, you are securing a positive cashflow rather than having the anxieties associated with waiting for cash receipts to cover cash disbursements. If that business has the ideal one-of-a-kind location, it may offer an opportunity you could not have if you were to start a business and had to wait for an acceptable location to become available. If you believe that an opportunity exists for starting a new business of the same type, for the same target market, and the same geographic area as the business you are considering buying, then one of the benefits of buying rather than starting a business is that there will be one less competitor.

Buying an existing business has at least four other potential advantages. First, an existing business has a financial track record. This may make it easier to attract debt financing and investors. This may be particularly important if it is a novel type of business. People are less willing to finance an unusual idea. However, they may be interested in investing in a proven unique business. The seller of the business also may be willing to provide financing assistance. In many instances, the seller's terms may be better than with any conventional lender. Buying an existing business thereby offers a financing alternative that is not available when a business is started from scratch. Second, in some cases, you may be able to acquire the assets you need for less money than if you had to buy all of them new when you start a business. Third, if the business has been successful, then either the owner or manager has been making the right decisions. If you do not have the level of experience necessary to manage the business, then you may be able to arrange a contract where the seller stays on as a consultant to teach you the ropes for a few months after you purchase the business. If the business has been managed by someone other than the owner, that person may be interested in staying on.

If you do not have enough money to buy the business, you may consider asking if the manager would be interested in investing in the business or becoming a partner. This could be a mutually advantageous proposition. You may need additional capital and management capability. This approach enables the manager to stay on the job. You may not own 100 percent of the business, but you will have a higher probability of making a profit. Some people may ask how you can afford to have the manager and yourself on the payroll. The answer is that if you buy and manage the business yourself, you will be spending most of your time learning the business. If you keep the manager, then the two of you can both concentrate on how to strengthen and expand the business.

Another advantage to buying a business is that the existing business may have unique features or exclusive assets. As noted earlier, if the existing business includes a facility (either owned or with a lease you can assume) that no one else can match, then buying that business provides a competitive advantage that would not be possible if you were to start that type of business from scratch. The same could also be true for the name of the business, its logo, if it has exclusive territorial rights to a popular brand, or if it has a patent or license privileges.

In some cases, it would be impossible, extremely time-consuming, or cost-prohibitive for you to try to develop these advantages from scratch. If so, it may be better to buy an existing business. Conversely, if you believe that you can create a competitive advantage, achieve superior financial performance, and do it with less capital, then you should start a new business rather than purchase an existing one. In many cases, first-timers will have a better chance of beating the odds if they buy an existing business.

Some Businesses Are for Sale, Others Can Be Bought

There are over 16 million businesses in the United States. Over 90 percent of these businesses are small businesses. At one time or another, nearly every owner thinks about selling the business. The average business changes hands every four years. The "businesses for sale" section of the classified ads and the listings by business brokers reflect only the tip of the iceberg. As one entrepreneur put it, "My business isn't for sale, but if someone comes along with the right offer, I'll sell it!" Ironically, some of the businesses listed for sale may not really be for sale. Some owners periodically list their businesses as a matter of curiosity to see if someone bites!

At least 20 percent of existing businesses are formally or informally up for sale. For every business formally listed, there may be two or three businesses of that type in your geographic area that could be purchased. This rule of thumb tells you it may be worth your while to check the network of people who know which businesses can be bought but are not formally on the market. Attorneys, loan officers, accountants, and trust officers are frequently aware of their clients' interests in selling their businesses. You may even consider running the classified ad "want to buy a business" that describes your interests in generic terms. If you are willing to move, then it may be worthwhile to contact Buyout Publications, Inc. This firm lists businesses for sale in various locations. If you are thinking about buying a midsized business, then you should contact NEBOR Publishing, Ltd. (301 Daniel Webster Highway in Marrimack, NH 03054). NEBOR publishes *The Business Opportunity Exchange* each month. This directory profiles over 5000 business acquisition opportunities throughout the United States.

There are about as many reasons why owners want to sell their businesses as there are businesses for sale. Unfortunately, many of the reasons given are not the real reasons that owners want to sell their business. The reasons for selling include: retirement, health problems, the desire to live in a different location, their sons or daughters do not want to take over the business, etc. In some cases, these may be the real reasons. In other cases, they are merely socially acceptable smoke screens to cover the real reason: the business is in trouble or the future is not very promising. Every business may be unique, but the following seven categories represent most of the businesses for sale:

1. Successful businesses with the potential to continue to be at least as prosperous.
2. Businesses that have been successful but have diminishing potential.
3. Businesses that have been moderately successful that have the potential to be very successful.
4. Businesses that have been moderately successful that are likely to continue their "lukewarm" existence.
5. Businesses that have been moderately successful, but are destined to decline and ultimately fail.
6. Businesses that have experienced difficulties but have the potential to stand on their own feet.
7. Businesses that have experienced difficulties and are destined to fail even if new management and additional funds are injected into them.

Businesses in the first, third, and sixth categories are worth considering. The fourth category may be acceptable if you are not ambitious. Owners of businesses in the second category usually want as much money as the first category of business. Many sellers in the fifth and seventh categories are anxious to find a buyer while there is something left to sell. If you are considering buying a business that has had problems, recognize that it may be more difficult to turn a troubled business around than to start one from scratch.

The sale of a business is similar to the sale of a stock certificate. The buyer is more optimistic about the future than the seller. The moral to this situation is that you may ask sellers the reasons why they want to sell, but perform a thorough investigation of the business, its market, and other related factors to be sure you are not about to buy a lemon. Also, if it seems to be too good a deal to be true, it probably is a deal you should pass up. Occasionally a business can be bought for a fraction of its worth because of a death or illness, but these situations are rare. When a business is for sale because of illness or death, realize that troubled businesses frequently contribute to health problems. Make sure the business you buy won't put you in the same predicament within a couple of years.

There are at least four other rules of thumb to keep in mind when you consider buying a business. First, you should develop a "target business profile." Before you go looking for a business to buy, you should have a specific set of criteria for what you expect. You need to identify how much you are willing to invest in a business, what level of risk you are willing to accept, what minimum return on investment you are willing to receive, and how much time you are willing to commit to learning and managing the business. Second, resist the temptation to buy the first business that looks good. Too often, people are so anxious to get into business that they buy the first one that comes along. This is particularly true if the business has considerable emotional appeal. If this happens to you, force yourself to step back and look at it objectively. Don't let the seller play the car salesperson's game of pressuring you to make an offer on the spot because someone else is also interested. Experience shows that people who maintain some objectivity and have patience find the right business. You should pursue buying a business with at least as much deliberation as a person would exercise when considering marrying someone. Emotions obviously will be a factor, but staying power should be a high priority.

The third rule of thumb applies to looking at businesses which have been around long enough to have a track record. Most businesses will not make a profit in their first year. If the business is not operating at least at its breakeven level by the end of its second year, then it may never make a profit. Moreover, a business that does not have a positive cashflow may need additional financing after you purchase it. A business with a positive cashflow will help you meet the financial obligations incurred in buying it.

You should concentrate your attention on businesses that have been operating for at least two years. The fact that a business has its head above water after two years is no guarantee it will continue to be profitable, but you will be increasing your odds of buying a business with a future. Someone once said, "It may take two years to know if you have a lemon, but it takes an oyster seven years to produce a pearl."

The fourth rule of thumb adopts the sky divers' motto, "Don't jump from the plane without a good parachute!" The same applies to buying a business. Make sure each business you consider buying can be sold if you find you were not meant to run a business or if you find it doesn't have as rosy a future as you thought. Check to see how long that business has been for sale and what price or financing "adjustments" had to be made to induce you to buy it. Make sure you are buying a business with a future rather than getting stuck with a liability.

Guidelines for Analyzing a Prospective Business

If you find a business that appears to be able to create and maintain customers and matches your capabilities, then you will need to do a thorough analysis to determine its real merit. The time has come to go beyond your initial impressions. Now you have to roll up your sleeves and look at the business from every possible angle.

The purchase of a business involves numerous players. The seller may be represented by a business broker. The seller will also consult with an accountant, an attorney, and investors in setting the asking price as well as negotiating the final terms of the sale. You should go into the process with your accountant, an attorney experienced in business buyouts, and a good idea of what you and the other investors are willing to commit to buying the business.

If a business broker is involved in listing the business you are pursuing, then that person should be able to provide you with the asking price, whether the owner is willing to provide financing assistance, what the terms of the sale and financing will be, a list of the assets and liabilities involved in the business, as well as an income statement and balance sheet for the past 12 months. Some business brokers are not willing to provide the financial information unless you make an initial offer to show your sincerity. This offer may simply involve signing a statement of confidentiality and disclosing certain personal and financial information.

Some brokers may ask for an earnest deposit before they will provide any financial information. They want to deal with qualified buyers. The practice of asking the inquirer to sign a statement of confidentiality and, in some instances, expecting a deposit does two things. First, it protects the seller from casual inquiries in which people, including competitors, can gain access to the seller's confidential financial information. Second, the statement and deposit indicate that the prospective buyer has the financial wherewithal to buy the business if the deliberations result in a formal offer. At first glance, this appears to be a tedious and cumbersome process, but it makes sense when you realize it may take three or more months to close a deal, even if it goes fairly smoothly. The broker minimizes casual window-shopping by expecting a tangible commitment from a prospective buyer early in the process. The deposit, if required, may be refunded under certain conditions.

The Book Value Approach to Valuing a Business

At this point, your major concern is determining what the business is worth. Unfortunately, there is no universally accepted formula for determining business worth. The traditional approach for setting selling price has been to take the book value or possibly the market value of the business's tangible assets and to add a certain amount for "goodwill." Goodwill represents the intangible side of the business. A successful business is more than the sum of its assets. As stated earlier, an ongoing business has an established name, a set of customers, an ongoing relationship with suppliers, a group of experienced employees, and so forth. Goodwill can be viewed as the price for reducing the amount of trial and error. It also reduces the risk associated with starting a business from scratch.

The value of goodwill and its bearing on the asking price represent the most emotional and controversial dimensions associated with purchasing a business. Sellers place a premium on the value of their business's goodwill. It reflects their contribution to the business. Buyers are savvy to the importance of goodwill; however, they usually prefer to have their money allocated to assets such as inventory and equipment, which can be converted into sales and depreciated to enhance cashflow.

The traditional approach to valuing a business concentrates on the business's balance sheet. The book value of the assets and goodwill are important because when most small businesses are sold, the buyer purchases the assets and the seller uses the proceeds of the sale to pay off the business's liabilities.

Even though there may be varying opinions on how to value goodwill, valuing the tangible assets is fairly straightforward. The current balance sheet reflects the book value of the assets. Book value represents the assets' original purchase price less accumulated depreciation.

If the current market or replacement value of the assets is greater than the book value, then the market value of the assets may be used to set the asking price instead of book value. Just as there are cases in which the market value exceeds the book value of the assets, there can also be instances when the assets are worth less than their book value.

You will need to have your accountant check the true value of the assets. Your accountant will pay particular attention to the percentage of accounts receivable that can be collected, whether the inventory is seasonal or out-of-date, and if the accumulated depreciation truly reflects the change in the value of the equipment. Your accountant will probably request that an audit be conducted. If the business has a substantial amount of assets or if the assets are unusual, it may be advisable to have a professional appraiser estimate the market value of the assets. In either case, it is advisable for you to choose the auditor or appraiser.

The value of goodwill may range from 10 or 20 percent of the value of the tangible assets to a multiple of their dollar value. If the business has not made money or if the assets and employees can be matched easily, then the goodwill may have minimal value. In other businesses, particularly service businesses, the value of goodwill may exceed the value of the tangible assets.

Two of the most valuable components of a service business are its customers and its employees. Service businesses such as insurance agencies, realty offices, beauty salons, and so on, do not have much in the way of tangible assets. The owners of service businesses are selling their "book of accounts." Service businesses are actually selling their customers. Their customers are their goodwill. If you were to start one of these businesses from scratch, you might be able to match an existing business's tangible assets, but it could take thousands of dollars of advertising and years of effort, among other things, to develop a comparable customer base. Even with an investment of this much time and money there is no guarantee that you could match the existing business. It is for this reason that you should have the seller sign a "noncompete and confidentiality" agreement as part of the sale of the business to you.

The traditional "assets plus goodwill" approach to establishing the asking price has its merits. It also has some drawbacks. Even if you can decide the best way to value the assets, you still have to determine the appropriate value of the business's goodwill.

The Capitalization-of-Earnings Approach to Valuing a Business

The more popular "capitalization-of-earnings" approach to valuing a business looks at the business's income statement more than its balance sheet. The major difference between the two methods is that the traditional approach's emphasis is on buying the assets of the business. The capitalization-of-earnings approach is concerned with buying the business's present and future profit potential. This approach has gained acceptance because two of the most important questions for the prospective buyer are, "What level of profit is the business presently generating?" and "What is it capable of generating?" Assets are important, but they are merely the means to an end—generating a profit. The business is valued according to what it is capable of doing rather than the assets it has on hand at the time of the sale.

The capitalization-of-earnings approach is consistent with the prospective buyer's interests. While the seller may want to get the equity out, the prospective buyer wants to know what level of return can be expected from investing in the business. Unfortunately, the capitalization-of-earnings approach has two major challenges. First, you need to determine the business's true profitability. Second, you need to determine the appropriate capitalization "rate" to apply to the earnings.

The capitalization-of-earnings approach to determining the value of the business is based on the following formula:

True net income × capitalization rate = value of business

This approach requires that the business's true net income be determined. Most first-timers assume that the net income from the last 12 months as reported on the business's income statement is an accurate figure. This figure may not always reflect the business's true profitability.

If the business is a proprietorship or a partnership, profit is defined as what is left after all the expenses are deducted from revenue. The business's profit actually represents what the owner gets for working at the business. The following example illustrates the point: The sole proprietor of a retail shop asked a consultant to give her an idea of what she should ask for her business if she were to put it up for sale. The consultant's first question was, "How much money did your business make in the last 12 months?" The owner said the business made $10,000. This sounded like a good return for a business with only $80,000 in sales.

The capitalization-of-earnings approach might use a rate of 4 for this business and yield the following value:

$$\text{Profit of } \$10,000 \times 4 = \$40,000$$

Herein lies one of the reasons why you need to be certain the profit figure in the formula reflects the true level of profit for the business. When you are valuing a proprietorship or partnership, you need to be sure that the figure represents profit after wages for the owner have been deducted.

The $10,000 profit figure should be modified to reflect the 40 hours a week for the 50 weeks the owner worked at the business during the last 12 months. If the owner were to have been paid a modest $5 per hour, then $10,000 ($5 × 2000 hours) should have been deducted from sales revenue as an operating expense. Wages for every employee, including the owner, must be deducted as an expense for a corporation. The same adjustment should be used if you are valuing a proprietorship or partnership. If the owner had not worked there, someone else would have been needed to do those tasks. The cost of labor, whoever it may be, needs to be reflected when determining true profitability.

If the $10,000 for the owner's time and effort is deducted from the previously reported $10,000 profit, it will provide the following value for the business:

$$\text{Profit of } \$0 \times 4 = \$0 \text{ value for the business}$$

At this point, you should say, "Wait a minute. Even though the business did not make a profit, it must be worth something." Obviously the business is worth something. It may not be making a true profit, but its balance sheet indicated $20,000 in assets and no liabilities.

In this instance, the owner should use the "assets plus goodwill" approach for figuring the asking price. The minimum asking price for a business should be the market value of its assets. An asking price of $24,000 was recommended for the retail business.

This price included $4000, or 20 percent of the assets, for goodwill. The business may not have made a profit, but it had an established set of customers and three more years of an assumable lease for a location that could not be matched.

The business was sold in four months for $21,000. The owner agreed to make a $3000 concession because the buyer's accountant determined that some of the inventory was seasonal. The owner also accepted the offer because the buyer was prepared to pay cash. This was important because the seller did not want to provide financing. The fact that the seller was anxious to move to Florida also expedited the sale.

This example may not be typical, but it illustrates the complexity of determining the actual level of profit and the true value of business assets. If the business had been profitable, then the capitalization-of-earnings approach may have been more appropriate. The capitalization rate, or multiple, is the most important part of the equation. If the business is profitable and has the potential to be even more profitable, then its present profit level will be multiplied by a higher capitalization rate. If it is a moderately profitable business and it is expected to continue being stable or lukewarm for the next few years because it is in a stagnant market or because competition will be increasing, then a lower capitalization rate will be used.

The capitalization rate and the value of goodwill used in the book value approach are similar. If the business is more profitable than comparable businesses, then it must have some advantage. The more profitable it is, the greater the value given to goodwill or the higher the capitalization rate.

The capitalization-of-earnings approach is similar to the approach used by most investors in the stock market. Investors in stock frequently use the price-earnings ratio for determining an appropriate price. If the business is making $4 per share and the business is expected to double its profits within four years, then investors may be willing to pay more for the stock than a company with less potential. In this case, investors may apply a capitalization rate of 6 to the $4-per-share profit. Thus, they would be willing to pay up to $24 a share for this business. If the business was not expected to do better, it may warrant a capitalization of 3. Investors would not be willing to pay more than $12 for a share of this business.

The capitalization rate places considerable weight on future profit potential. Capitalization rates may be as low as 2 or as high as 20, depending on how long the business has been operating, market growth, competitive response, and the present profit level. In a start-up business, there is no profit, so future profits become the basis for what a person may be willing to invest in the business. An existing business has financial statements that reflect present and past profitability.

The following example demonstrates how the capitalization approach can be used in valuing an established and profitable business. A wholesaler of plumbing fixtures wanted to sell his business. He was 65 years old and planned to retire in the coming year. He started the business 30 years earlier and it had grown into the leading wholesale business for plumbing fixtures in the area. The asking price for the business was set at $400,000.

The prospective buyer for the business had experience in manufacturing plumbing fixtures and wanted to relocate in that area. The prospective buyer requested the financial statements for the last five years. The prospective buyer's accountant reviewed the figures and brought in a professional appraiser to determine the true value of the assets.

The business was a corporation and had no long-term debt. The income statement for the past 12 months indicated that the business had a pretax profit of $75,000. The previous income statements revealed that the business had averaged $60,000 in profit for each of the four preceding years. The appraiser valued the assets, which included inventory, fixtures, equipment, supplies, receivables, metal building, and land, at $280,000. This meant the owner wanted $120,000 for goodwill.

At this point, the prospective buyer had to decide whether to: (1) make an offer, (2) try to start a similar business from scratch, (3) look for a similar business to buy, or (4) look for a different opportunity. The prospective buyer made an offer for $360,000. The offer was based on the following rationale. First, the area had considerable growth potential. Housing starts were increasing and the trend was expected to continue for the next few years. Second, even though the prospective buyer may have been able to match the assets for $280,000 by starting from scratch, he knew he would be at a competitive disadvantage to the existing businesses. Third, this business had an established relationship with plumbing contractors in the area. Fourth, the business had exclusive regional distribution rights for the leading brand of plumbing fixtures. Fifth, the prospective buyer wanted to hire the general manager to run the business while he learned the ropes. The general manager was considered excellent and was interested in staying on following the transfer of ownership. Sixth, the business had an extensive inventory of plumbing fixtures that were no longer being manufactured. These fixtures were valuable because homes and other buildings that had been built 30 years earlier now needed replacement fixtures. This business was the only wholesaler in the area with these items in inventory.

The steady stream of profits, the large amount of goodwill, and the potential improvement in profitability provided the basis for extending the offer. The owner, however, rejected the offer. He knew the business was worth $400,000 and was not willing to negotiate.

The buyer had made the original offer of $360,000 because he was not looking for the owner to provide financing assistance. The prospective buyer was also "fishing" to see if the owner would be willing to accept 10 percent less than the asking price.

The prospective buyer returned a week later with an offer of $400,000. He had no reservation about offering $400,000 for the business, because the capitalization-of-earnings approach indicated it was worth at least that price. The capitalization formula indicated:

$$\frac{\$400,000 \text{ asking price}}{\$75,000 \text{ current profit}} = 5.33 \text{ capitalization rate}$$

This rate of capitalization would be appropriate for a business that is generating a good return and has a promising future. If the business was to continue earning $75,000 each year, then it would be generating an 18.75 percent return on the $400,000 investment. This would be a very good investment.

The prospective buyer considered the future to be even brighter than the present. He also felt the business warranted a capitalization rate of 7 or 8. The prospective buyer felt the business would have been a good deal even at 7 times $75,000, or $525,000! The irony of this situation was that the prospective buyer believed that the $75,000 profit did not reflect the firm's real profit for the past 12 months. The income statements indicated that the owner had taken $60,000 out of the business as the "president's salary" for each of the past five years. This amount was recorded as an expense, not as a dividend. The prospective buyer felt this produced an understatement of earnings, because the owner lived in another state and was barely involved in business operations. The buyer would not expect to draw that large a salary. He also planned to use part of the $60,000 to make it lucrative for the general manager to stay and teach the buyer the ropes. The prospective buyer figured the business's true profitability for the last year to be closer to $95,000 or $100,000. This meant that even if a conservative capitalization rate of 4 was used, the business was worth at least $400,000.

The capitalization-of-earnings approach can be summarized as, "How much money are you willing to pay to buy a certain level of earnings?" In the preceding case, the prospective buyer was willing to pay $400,000 to buy a $100,000 return. At this price, he would be getting a 25 percent ($100,000 divided by $400,000) return on his investment. This was a very good deal and it had the potential to be even better. But this offer was also turned down. The seller concluded that the business was worth more than the $400,000 asking price. The seller took it off the market because the business would serve as an excellent pension vehicle for him.

Closing the Sale: Don't Forget
Your Accountant and Attorney

Buying a business involves more than just agreeing on the selling price. You will need to have the advice of your accountant and attorney on numerous aspects of the purchase agreement.

Your accountant will need to review the financial records and tax returns for the last few years. She or he will be trying to determine the accuracy of the records and developing a clear picture of the business's revenues, expenses, profits, assets, and liabilities. Your accountant will also be in a position to help you make financial projections for the next two or three years. You should pay particular attention to the cashflow. Hopefully, the business will be able to generate enough cash to meet the financial obligations you will incur in buying it.

Your attorney will play a major role in helping you establish the terms for purchasing the business. Your attorney will be involved in:

1. Checking to see if there are any liens on the business's assets or chattel mortgages.
2. Drafting a noncompete and confidentiality clause for the seller to sign.
3. Establishing an indemnity agreement in which the seller agrees to protect the buyer from any claims made by creditors.
4. Making sure that an escrow account is set up by the seller to cover any claims.
5. Having the seller sign an affidavit, indicating that all creditors have been notified of the sale of the business.
6. Drafting a clause in which the seller guarantees all accounts receivable.
7. Checking to see that all leases can be assumed.
8. Making sure all warranties, contracts, and sales agreements by the seller are known.
9. Having the seller indicate that no litigation or government investigation is currently under way.
10. Checking on the status of all license agreements, patents, customer lists, recipes, formulas, processes, copyrights, logos, etc.
11. Reviewing all zoning requirements and permits.
12. Drafting a casualty clause whereby the buyer can get out of the agreement if there is a major calamity such as a fire or flood that

affects the future of the business before the title to the business is formally transferred.

13. Establishing the final terms for the sale of the business. This includes the listing of the assets, including serial numbers (where applicable), the liabilities to be assumed, how inventory and accounts receivable adjustments will be made, as well as the actual date and conditions for completing the sale.

Your attorney will also establish certain conditions to ensure that the seller continues doing business as usual up to the date of sale. It is important that goodwill with customers, suppliers, creditors, and employees not be allowed to deteriorate. Your attorney also may put a clause in the purchase agreement whereby any disputes after the sale between the buyer and seller will be handled by the American Arbitration Association, if the two parties are unable to resolve them.

It should be obvious that buying a business takes a lot of time, knowledge, and patience. You must have a good idea of what you are looking for and what you are willing to do to buy a business. In many cases, it is easier, quicker, and better to buy an existing business than to start one from scratch. But remember, there are no guarantees. Just because the business has done well is no assurance that you or anyone else will make a profit. If you are thinking about buying a business, be sure the three basic ingredients are present: (1) a market exists where customers are in search of a business, (2) you have the ability to make the right decisions to create and maintain customers, and (3) there is a sufficient financial return to justify the risk.

11
Acquiring a Franchise

Buying Someone Else's Formula for Success

People are often frustrated because they lack the experience and skills to start a business from scratch. When they consider buying an existing business, they either feel like they are buying a used car or they do not want to be limited to the businesses available for sale. Fortunately, there may be a happy medium. Franchises offer the excitement of starting one's own business while reducing the trial-and-error process experienced by most first-timers.

There are over two thousand organizations that offer franchise rights in the United States. Franchises are available for nearly every type of business. If you are considering the retail market where businesses sell goods or services to the ultimate consumer, then a franchise may be a good way to get into business. Franchises account for one-third to one-half of all retail sales in the United States. Whether you believe a market opportunity exists for chimney sweeping, residential landscaping, parking lot striping, or operating a fitness center, there is at least one franchise available to help you beat the odds.

When you buy a franchise, you are buying someone's "formula for success." This is similar to the reason why many people buy an existing business. Buying a franchise is like buying "goodwill." Two of the major strengths of a franchise are: (1) most franchises have already tried their business idea in the marketplace to see if they could create and maintain customers for a profit and (2) the franchisors have developed a formula for improving the chances of being successful.

The failure rate for people who purchase a franchise is much lower than for independent business start-ups. Nearly 40 percent of nonfranchise start-ups fail in the first year of operation. Less than 5 percent of franchises are discontinued after one year. If you use a 10-year time frame, four out of five independent businesses no longer exist. Only one out of five franchises fail. While there is no guarantee that every franchise—even a McDonald's—will succeed, the track record makes a case for considering the franchise route. The benefits of a franchise are particularly noteworthy if you have limited experience.

In many cases, the franchising company, or "franchisor," has been operating that type of business for at least two or three years. During that time, the franchisor has developed an understanding for what does and does not work. Franchises thereby offer the first-timer the opportunity to "hit the ground running." The franchisee does not have to take the time and risk associated with reinventing the wheel.

The Benefits of Buying a Franchise

The franchisor sells a license which offers the franchisee certain rights and privileges. The privileges can vary dramatically among franchises, even in the same industry. In some cases, the franchisee has the opportunity to receive management assistance and to buy supplies and inventory at favorable prices from the franchisor. In a few cases, the franchisee can buy a complete business package. The franchisee purchases all the supplies, fixtures and equipment, inventory, and even the building and land from the franchisor.

The most significant advantage of buying a franchise is that the franchisor has developed a "formula for success." This explains why franchises have been so popular in the past 20 years. As noted in the beginning of this book, the number-one reason for small business failure is the lack of management experience and education.

The most successful franchises offer a well-developed formula as well as training programs for the franchisee and his or her employees. The training programs and other forms of management assistance usually cover various aspects of opening and operating the franchise. The formula and training may not guarantee success, but they usually provide the first-timer with a higher probability of being successful than simply starting an independent business from scratch.

Most franchises offer numerous other benefits. The franchisor may help the franchisee select the appropriate site for the business, provide centralized purchasing to take advantage of quantity discounts, and offer a computerized accounting system to simplify paperwork. Franchisors often provide cooperative advertising arrangements whereby the franchisor subsidizes a portion of the franchisee's advertising. Franchisors frequently provide franchisees with prepared artwork for their advertising. This enhances the quality of the franchisee's advertising and reduces the expense for artwork.

Some franchisors send specialists to help the franchisee with the grand opening of the business and stay on the scene to help the franchisee through the first week or two. These franchises usually have "circuit riders" who visit franchisees on a periodic basis to provide additional management assistance. Some franchisors also provide newsletters that offer ideas on how to improve various aspects of the business. A few franchises even offer a "franchise hotline" to provide answers to pressing questions.

A number of franchisors will provide trade data and help franchisees prepare financial projections when they apply for a loan. A few franchises even offer direct financing to qualified franchisees.

The Drawbacks of Buying a Franchise

The saying, "There is no free lunch" applies to the franchise concept. Franchisees learn the franchisor's formula for success and receive other privileges in return for franchise fees and various restrictions.

Franchisees pay one or more franchise fees to secure the right to conduct business under the franchisor's name. This may be viewed more as a trade-off than a drawback. Nevertheless, you need to recognize that it may take more money to buy a franchise than to start a business from scratch. Franchise fees will increase your initial capital requirement and affect your income statement.

The initial "franchise" fee represents the most common fee paid by franchisees. The franchisee pays a specific amount of money for the right to use the franchise name. This fee may range from a few hundred dollars for a new service-type franchise to over one hundred thousand dollars for a leading hotel franchise. A few franchisors do not charge a franchise fee or they waive it as a special promotion to generate interest.

Quite a few people are attracted to franchises with low initial franchise fees. These people get excited because the low fee means that it will not cost a lot of money to start their business as a franchise. Two popular sayings may be worth noting when reviewing the initial franchise fee for various franchises. The first saying is, "You get what you pay for." In many instances, the franchise fee merely lets you use the franchise's name on your business card, letterhead, yellow-page ad, and sign. The franchisor may not provide any other benefits or assistance. A rule of thumb for initial franchise fees is that the more established and successful the franchise, the higher the initial franchise fee. The initial franchise fee is like goodwill. If the franchise is going to provide you with a competitive edge and a higher probability of making a profit, then you should be willing to pay for that advantage.

It is not unusual for a new franchise to have a very low initial franchise fee. When a franchise is being established, the franchisor usually incurs considerable expense in legal, promotional, and accounting fees, not to mention the overhead associated with the franchise team's salary-related expenses.

New franchisors are so eager to get some money back into their checking accounts and to have a few franchises be the lead dominos to show that the formula works that they will offer the first franchisees a low initial franchise fee. A restaurateur once told the story of how a franchisor called him one night and offered him the exclusive rights in two states for a new fast-food hamburger franchise for just $10,000. The restaurateur turned down the offer because he thought there already were too many hamburger franchises. This restaurateur will regret his decision for the rest of his life. That hamburger franchise is now one of the top ten fast-food franchises in the country. There are over one hundred locations in those two states. He would have become a multimillionaire within five years by merely selling franchise rights for various locations in the two states.

While this is not the typical situation, it does illustrate that the franchise fee is usually a product of supply and demand. When there are only a few franchisees, the fee may be low, but as more people want that franchise, the fees increase in proportion to the demand.

The second saying, "Look before you leap," encourages the prospective franchisee to put things in perspective. The franchisor can make money in only three ways. The franchisor can make money by selling franchise rights, collecting ongoing fees, or doing a combination of these two. If the initial franchise fee is very low, then the franchisor usually has a higher fee structure for the "operational" side of being a franchisee.

Operational fees may come in various forms. The most common operational fee is the royalty fee. The royalty fee usually is a percentage of the franchisee's sales. In some franchise agreements, the percentage rate will fluctuate with the level of sales. The royalty percentage tends to be between 2 and 6 percent of sales.

First-timers frequently express concern about acquiring a franchise when they learn about the royalty fee. They ask, "Why isn't the royalty fee taken out of profits rather than sales?" The answer is short and simple: Franchisors want their money right off the top; it's up to the franchisee to make a profit.

First-timers also wonder if it is worth being a franchisee if they have to pay the franchisor a percentage of sales. They view the royalty fee as an expense that independent businesses do not have to pay. After all, if the average business's profit is less than 4 percent of sales, then how can a franchise make a profit if it has to pay a 5 percent royalty fee?

The best way to view this situation is to ask yourself, "Is my business going to have a significantly higher level of sales because the franchise will have name recognition?" and, "Will I have better training than is found in independent businesses?" The prospective franchisee also needs to ask, "Will my other expenses be lower than an independent business's expenses because the franchisor provides me with economies in recordkeeping, supplies, fixtures and equipment, and so on?" If so, then the royalty fee may be justified.

The second most common operating fee is the advertising fee. Most franchisees pay a percentage of their sales to the franchisor for regional and national advertising. This fee also enables the franchisor to sponsor franchisewide sales promotions. Franchisors recognize the need for their franchisees to be visible in the marketplace. Anyone who has children who watch television will acknowledge that fast-food franchises own Saturday mornings. Most of the commercials are designed to have the children who are viewing the cartoon shows want to go to at least one of the franchises sometime during the weekend, if not that morning!

Some first-timers have mixed emotions about paying the advertising fee. Research has shown that independent businesses tend to be reluctant to spend much money on advertising. It has also shown that when they do spend money on advertising, it tends to be done in a haphazard manner.

It has been said that you have to spend money to make money. This definitely applies to advertising—provided that you spend it wisely. The advertising fee makes sense because it keeps franchisees from short-changing their advertising budgets. It also means that franchisees will have professionally researched and prepared advertising packages.

Franchisees benefit from the franchisor's economies of scale. The franchisor can secure regional and national television time and magazine space at lower rates than small independent businesses. The same applies for radio spots and graphic art.

Two other aspects of franchise advertising are worth noting. Most franchisors expect, and in many cases require, that each franchisee spend a certain percentage of sales on local advertising and sales promotions each year. Some franchisors have an interesting approach to handling the advertising fee. They use part of the advertising fee to subsidize each franchisee's local advertising expenses. For every dollar of local advertising, the franchisor may rebate a certain percent. This is the franchisor's way of encouraging franchisees to advertise more extensively than their local competitors.

Franchisors want to establish automatic name association. When potential customers think of food, McDonald's wants customers in search of a business to think "McDonald's." When a couple is thinking about selling their house, Century 21 wants them to think "Century 21." The same applies to pizza and Domino's, printing and PIP, ice cream and Baskin-Robbins, as well as mufflers and Midas. In the competitive marketplace, franchisees often overwhelm independent businesses with their advertising.

There are a few other franchise-related fees. They are referred to as the "hidden" fees. Franchisees may have to purchase all their equipment, supplies, and inventory from the franchisor. In some cases, the franchisee may be required to buy the building and the land from the franchisor. The franchisor may charge the franchisee a monthly fee for maintaining the franchisee's records on a computerized accounting system. The franchisee may also be required to travel to and pay a registration fee to attend franchisor-sponsored training meetings.

Franchisors receive quantity discounts from vendors when they buy fixtures, equipment, inventory, and supplies. They may pass some of their economies of scale to their franchisees. Conversely, they can make a profit from these items when they sell them to the franchisees. If the franchisor passes the discounts on to the franchisee, then the franchisee may have a considerable cost advantage over competitors. If not, the added costs of doing business as a franchisee may make it difficult for the franchisee to make a profit.

Franchise agreements that require franchisees to buy various goods and services exclusively from the franchisor reflect the monopoly power of some franchisors. These restrictions represent the second major drawback of being a franchisee. As noted earlier, when a person acquires a franchise, that person is buying a "formula" for success. While the formula has its benefits, prospective franchisees need to recognize that it may be a formula they won't be able to change. Franchise formulas almost always have numerous restrictions attached to them.

These restrictions may include: (1) whether the franchisee must operate the franchise unit, (2) whether the franchisee can own more than one unit or any other business, (3) the hours the unit must be open, (4) the prices to charge customers, (5) the location for the franchise, (6) the design of the building, (7) what goods and services can be sold, and (8) who the franchisee can sell the franchise to. These restrictions are the franchisor's way of increasing the franchisee's likelihood of success. Franchisors establish these guidelines to assure consistency from one franchisee to another. At one time, Holiday Inn used this consistency as the basis for its advertising campaign. Holiday Inn's television spots stated, "At Holiday Inns, there are no surprises. You can expect the same quality rooms and service at each location."

Some franchisees find the guidelines very constraining. Consistency has its merits, but each local marketplace has its own uniqueness. Every business endeavor, whether it is a franchise or an independent business, needs to tailor its market offering and operations to the particular needs and interests of its target market. Most fast-food franchisors do not allow their franchisees to create their own entrees or to add other popular items to their menus. McDonald's operated for over 20 years before they added chicken and ice cream to their menus. When salads became popular, many franchisees were frustrated. All they could do was watch their customers go to other restaurants to eat what McDonald's franchisees could easily have prepared on their own.

The restrictive nature of many franchise agreements prohibits franchisees from owning additional franchise units or other businesses. Some agreements stipulate that the franchisee must be present for at least 48 weeks of the year. This is constraining to some franchisees. It keeps them from capitalizing on other opportunities and from taking a lot of vacation time. A few franchisees have been known to exclaim, "I went into business so I could be my own boss; these restrictions do not permit me to make my own decisions."

As is true with most things in life, franchises involve compromises. Many people need the formula, the training, the management assistance, the advertising ideas, the computerized accounting system, and the standardized operating procedures. Franchises may represent the best way for inexperienced people to go into business. In a figurative sense, the franchisor acts as a senior partner.

Not everyone is cut out to be a franchisee. If you are the type of person who constantly identifies market opportunities, has extensive experience, and prefers flexibility and creativity over assistance and structure, then you may be better off starting your own business from scratch. If you are a very enterprising person and have the dream of doing things on a grand scale, then you should find an emerging market opportunity that will permit you to become a franchisor rather than a franchisee.

Finding the Right Franchise Opportunity

If you have come to the conclusion that the franchise route may be the best avenue to take to establish your own business, then the time has arrived to begin the process of searching for the most appropriate franchise. The process of selecting a franchise is similar to starting a business from scratch or buying an existing business. The process starts with identifying areas of opportunity, is followed with determining whether you have or can develop the capabilities to create and maintain customers, and is concluded with estimating whether there will be enough return to justify the time and money to be invested in the business.

The first step in finding the right franchise is to identify markets with growth opportunity and geographic areas where customers are in search of a business. Someone once said, "When looking for a house to buy, find a neighborhood where you would like to live and then look for a house you would like to have for your home." The same rationale applies when looking for a franchise.

The process of identifying the right franchise begins with identifying the right type of business. If you were planning to go sailing, you would find it easier to sail if the wind was to your advantage and the water was not rough. The nautical saying, "May you always have the wind at your back," is good advice for the prospective franchisee. It is easier to sail with the wind than against it. It is also better to check the weather report before setting sail. The forecast may indicate that the calm you see may merely be the calm before the storm.

Too many people are attracted to industries that are already saturated with competition. Under these conditions, it is difficult for any franchise to make a profit. A popular franchise in a saturated market may have less chance for being successful than an emerging franchise in a new market with greater potential.

The prospective franchisee needs to make a deliberate effort to keep his or her eyes and mind open for lasting business opportunities. All too often, people are impressed with the fame of international franchises or seduced by fads in which new franchises are formed that offer rags to riches within six months.

Even though most franchises have good track records, none can guarantee success. The prospective franchisee should be reminded of the saying, "It takes a good jockey and a good horse to win the race. No jockey has been known to win a race by carrying the horse across the finish line!" In this analogy, the horse is the marketplace and the jockey is the franchisee.

The prospective franchisee needs to answer two questions at this time. The first question is, "What is the best opportunity?" The second question is, "Which is the best franchise to help me capitalize on that opportunity?" You should refer back to Chapter 2, which describes the step-by-step process for identifying business opportunities. The only difference between the process discussed in that chapter and the process of acquiring a franchise is that once you have identified the top two or three opportunities, you will investigate the franchises available to determine which ones offer the capability to create and maintain customers for a profit.

If your market research reveals good opportunities in the areas of child care, residential landscaping, employment agencies, and printing services, then it is time to learn about the franchises available for each type of business. The first place to begin your investigation of available franchises is the nearest library. The following four books may be very helpful: *The Directory of Franchise Organizations*, published by Pilot Industries, Inc.; *The Franchise Annual*, published by In/O Franchise News; *The Source Book of Franchise Opportunities*, published by Dow-Jones Irwin, Inc.; and the *Franchise Opportunities Handbook*, published by the U. S. Department of Commerce. These books list each franchisor's address and phone number, the year the franchise was established, the number of operating franchise units, the number of franchisor-owned units, and the geographic areas served by the franchise. The books also contain information on the initial investment requirement, the fee structure, the average number of employees per unit, the services offered by the franchisor, if the franchisee has exclusive territorial rights, and whether the franchisor provides financial assistance. *The Rating Guide to Franchises*, by Dennis L. Foster, may also be helpful. It rates numerous franchises on various key dimensions. *Inc.* and other small business magazines also provide profiles of newly formed as well as established franchises.

The prospective franchisee should contact numerous franchisors in the fields that appear to have potential and ask them for a "franchise packet." Franchisors welcome the opportunity to send people information about their businesses.

The prospective franchisee should also contact the International Franchise Association (IFA) at 1025 Connecticut Avenue, N.W., in Washington, D.C. 20036. The IFA provides information about franchising and specific franchises. You should also go to your library and review the *Business Periodicals Index* and *The Magazine Index* for the past two years to learn what has been written about the franchises that interest you. The Better Business Bureau, Dun & Bradstreet, and the U.S. Small Business Administration may also be able to provide background information on various franchises. Your accountant, attorney, loan officer, and local chamber of commerce may also be in a position to assist you in investigating a franchise.

The next step is to review the information for the franchises that have initial appeal. Some of the franchises may be eliminated from consideration because they require a higher franchise fee than you can afford.

Other franchisors may not have territories or individual units available where you want to locate.

This step requires a fairly rigorous and objective analysis of each franchise. Your accountant can help you by reviewing the financial information in the franchise packet and from other sources. Your banker may check to see if your bank has done business with any franchisees and learn whether they are doing well.

Quite a few franchises will be dropped from your list of alternatives because they do not have good track records or because little information is available to review. This is why it may be advisable to consider only franchises that have been operating for at least four years. The chapter on buying a business stressed the need to review at least three years of financial records. One or two years of operating results may not provide sufficient information for determining the franchisee's profit potential.

Checking Out the Franchisors

At this point, you probably have narrowed your interest to four or five franchises. More than likely, the franchisors have called you to follow up on the franchise packet they sent to you. If not, it may be time to contact them. You should request specific information about the availability and terms for a franchise unit. You should also request a copy of the franchise agreement and any other contractual obligations between the franchisor and franchisee.

One of the advantages of buying a franchise rather than an existing business is that federal and state laws require franchisors to provide franchisees with a disclosure statement. Federal Trade Commission Rule 439 enacted in 1979 states that franchise units cannot be sold without disclosure statements. This statement must be provided at the first face-to-face meeting between the franchisor and franchisee. This legislation also stipulates that the franchisee must have the document at least 10 days prior to any exchange of money or before the franchisee signs the franchise agreement.

The disclosure statement contains a considerable amount of information on the background of the franchisor. The statement must identify the franchisor's officers, directors, and principal owners. Rule 439 also requires that any criminal convictions, civil judgments, bankruptcies, or administrative orders by or against these people be contained in the disclosure statement. The statement must also include a description of their business experience.

The disclosure statement must indicate the nature of the licensing agreement, the fees to be paid, the types of assistance the franchisor will provide, a description of any territorial protection for the franchisee, and the conditions affecting the sale or loss of franchise rights by the franchisee. The disclosure statement needs to include a copy of the franchisor's latest income statement and balance sheet. These financial records must have been audited by a CPA. The disclosure statement is not reviewed by the Federal Trade Commission, but the franchisor is liable for any errors. Franchisors are also required to substantiate any earnings figures they cite by their franchisees.

Numerous states require franchisors to provide franchisees with additional information or place other restrictions on the promotion and sale of franchise units. Prospective franchisees have far more information about franchise agreements and protection from unscrupulous or fly-by-night franchisors than when franchises started to gain popularity years ago. Nevertheless, you should not limit your investigation of franchises to the material required by federal and state guidelines.

The prospective franchisee should review the sales and profit figures for a cross section of existing franchisees. Do not rely only on the figures provided by the franchisor. Select a representative group of franchisees and visit them. You should observe their operations and ask each franchisee about what you might expect for financial results, competition, and assistance from the franchisor after you sign the agreement.

It may also be worthwhile to contact some of the people who sold their franchise units to learn why they sold their franchise rights. Suppliers of existing franchise units may also provide some interesting views on the value of that particular franchise. This would also be a good time to determine what avenues for recourse may be available to you if the franchisor fails to fulfill the terms of the franchise agreement.

Look Before You Leap

Franchises are an excellent avenue for beating the odds. Recent trade figures indicate that for three-quarters of the franchises in the United States, the franchisee failure rate is less than 5 percent. Yet it pays to be selective. Franchising is similar to a marriage. You should look for a franchise that will stand the test of time. If the franchisor goes under, you will be left in an awkward and lonely situation. To be successful, you will need a market opportunity that will last and a franchisor who will be there to help you create and maintain customers for a profit. The right franchise is the one that will strengthen your business venture without having you make too many sacrifices. How the franchisor deals with you in the courtship stage may serve as a barometer to the type of relationship and assistance you can expect during marriage.

The best way to review a franchise opportunity is to view it from all angles. Reviewing a franchise takes considerable effort. It also takes time and money. It may take four to six months from your initial inquiry to reach agreement on the final terms of the franchise contract. It may take an additional six months to open your business. It should be apparent that you will need to have your CPA, attorney, investors, and possibly your commercial loan officer with you from the beginning. These people will encourage you to look before you leap. They are also in a good position to give you professional advice on the relative merits of the franchises you are reviewing.

Index

About the Author

Stephen C. Harper is president of his own management consulting firm, Harper and Associates, Inc. He is also a professor of management at the University of North Carolina at Wilmington, where he directs that university's Small Business Institute. Harper is a frequent speaker and seminar presenter and has received special recognition for outstanding service from the U.S. Small Business Administration. His doctorate in management is from Arizona State University. He is the editor and coauthor of the book *Management: Who Ever Said It Would Be Easy?* (1983).